Que® Quick Reference Series

UNIX® Programmer's Quick Reference

John Valley

Que® Corporation
Carmel, Indiana

UNIX® Programmer's Quick Reference.

Library of Congress Catalog Number: 90-60180

ISBN 0-88022-535-1

93 92 91 90 5 4 3 2

Interpretation of the printing code: the rightmost double-digit number is the year of the book's printing; the rightmost single-digit number is the number of the book's printing. For example, a printing code of 89-4 shows that the fourth printing of the book occurred in 1989.

Information in this book is based on UNIX System V, Release 3.

Que Quick Reference Series

The *Que Quick Reference Series* is a portable resource of essential microcomputer knowledge. Whether you are a new or experienced user, you can rely on the high-quality information contained in these convenient guides.

Drawing on the experience of many of Que's best-selling authors, the *Que Quick Reference Series* helps you easily access important program information. Now it's easy to look up programming information for assembly language, C, DOS and BIOS functions, QuickBASIC 4, Turbo Pascal, and UNIX as well as frequently used commands and functions for 1-2-3, WordPerfect 5, MS-DOS, dBASE IV, and AutoCAD.

Use the *Que Quick Reference Series* as a compact alternative to confusing and complicated traditional documentation.

The *Que Quick Reference Series* also includes these titles:

1-2-3 Quick Reference
1-2-3 Release 2.2 Quick Reference
1-2-3 Release 3 Quick Reference
Assembly Language Quick Reference
AutoCAD Quick Reference
C Quick Reference
dBASE IV Quick Reference
DOS and BIOS Functions Quick Reference
Hard Disk Quick Reference
Harvard Graphics Quick Reference
MS-DOS Quick Reference
Microsoft Word 5 Quick Reference
Norton Utilities Quick Reference
PC Tools Quick Reference
QuickBASIC Quick Reference
Turbo Pascal Quick Reference
WordPerfect Quick Reference

Programming Books Director
Allen L. Wyatt, Sr.

Product Development Specialist
Linda Sanning

Managing Editor
Wendy Ford

Production Editor
Marj Hopper

Editor
Gail S. Burlakoff

Technical Editors
Jim Carr
Don Gloistein

Editorial Assistant
Ann K. Taylor

Trademark Acknowledgments

Que Corporation has made every effort to supply trademark information about company names, products, and services mentioned in this book. Trademarks indicated below were derived from various sources. Que Corporation cannot attest to the accuracy of this information.

UNIX is a registered trademark of AT&T.

Table of Contents

Introduction

The *UNIX Programmer's Quick Reference* is a concise summary of UNIX System V system calls and library functions for the C language programmer.

The book has two main sections: a *C Function Reference* and a section on *Principal Data Structures*. In the *C Function Reference*, which documents the most commonly used C library functions, entries are the function names themselves. Entries are arranged in strict alphabetical order; names beginning with an underscore precede those beginning with *a*. Unlike most other UNIX books, this book does not have entries such as *ctype* or *string*.

The *Principal Data Structures* section documents data structures that you must provide to, or which are supplied to you from, various system calls. Entries are the names of the header files that define the data structures; again, entries are in alphabetical order.

A *Function Finder* section is provided to help you find a function to meet a specific need.

Including the entire UNIX System V collection of C-language functions in this small volume would be impractical. Deciding which to omit has been difficult—a task guided chiefly by a desire to address the needs of most readers. While all UNIX functions are useful, we believe that many are not appropriate for developing general-purpose portable applications. Therefore, with a few exceptions, the functions omitted are those intended only for specialized applications, usable only by the super-user, or having a machine-dependent definition.

Table 1 lists the most notable functions excluded from this book. But be aware that the list cannot be complete because of the variety of currently available UNIX implementations.

Table 1. Other UNIX System V functions

a64l	l3tol	ldsseek	semctl
acct	l64a	ldtbindex	semget
brk	ldaclose	ldtbread	semop
chroot	ldahread	ldtbseek	setgrent
crypt	ldaopen	ltol3	setutent
dial	ldclose	mknod	sgetl encrypt
ldexp	monitor	shmat	endgrent
ldfhread	mount	shmctl	endutent
ldgetname	msgctl	shmdt	fgetgrent
ldlinit	msgget	shmget	fgetpwent
ldlitem	msgrcv	sputl	frexpldlread
msgsnd	ssignal	ftok	ldlseek
nlist	stime	getgrent	ldnrseek
plock	swab	getgrgid	ldnseek
profil	sync	getgrnam	ldnshread
ptrace	times	getpw	ldnsseek
putpwent	ttyslot	getutent	ldohseek
pututline	uadmin	getutid	ldopen
regcmp	umount	getutline	ldrseek
regex	ustat	gsignal	ldshread
sbrk	utmpname		

This book describes only selected entries from System V; it includes none of the functions unique to Release 4. The new features are often highly complex or of limited use, and implementation may vary from one version of System V to another. The functions listed here, a part of UNIX for many years, provide a sound basis for application development.

Notational Conventions

Occasionally, you will find a keyword below and to the right of the function name. These keywords highlight special usage considerations for the function; their meanings are explained in table 2.

Table 2. Usage Symbols

Keyword	*Meaning*
`errno`	Sets `errno` global
S	System call
KE	Requires Kernel Extensions
R3	Requires System V Release 3
`-lm`	`cc` option for math library
`-lmalloc`	`cc` option for `malloc` library
`-lPW`	`cc` option for auxiliary library

The `-l` keywords mark functions that are not part of the standard C function library; you must take special measures to use these functions. The procedure is simple: just include the indicated `-l` keyword on the **cc** command line, as in the following example:

```
cc myprog.c -lm -lPW -o myprog
```

In this example, the math library (`-lm`) and the auxiliary library (`-lPW`) must be searched in addition to the standard library.

In the body of a description, the arguments of a function are shown in italics; occasionally, italics are used also to identify technical terms special to UNIX.

A monospace font is used to indicate the names of functions (`read` or `wait`, for example), UNIX commands (`cc` or `find`), standard UNIX path or file names (`/etc/passwd` or `/usr/include`, for example), and the names of structs your program may reference. Sample code lines or fragments are shown not only in a monospace font, but they are highlighted in blue.

Warning

Be sure to pay special attention to notes marked like this. They are intended to warn you of ways programmers often misuse a function. Bugs arising from a misused function can be incredibly difficult to find despite powerful debuggers like `sdb`.

C Function Reference

The UNIX operating system provides many functions for C programmers. In UNIX, functions are stored in several libraries, some of which are intended for general programming, some for special purposes.The general-purpose C function libraries are described in this section.

A library is a collection of *object files* (files with names ending in *.o*) stored in a single file called an *archive*. Archives are created and maintained by using the `ar` command. The archive files listed in table 3 contain the general-purpose C function libraries; they are located in either the `/lib` or `/usr/lib` directories.

Table 3. Standard function libraries

File name	*Library usage*
`libc.a`	Standard C function library
`libm.a`	Math library
`libmalloc.a`	Malloc library
`libPW.a`	Auxiliary library

The standard library (`libc.a`) is always searched by the `cc` command. Functions in other libraries will be linked with your program only if the appropriate `-l` option is included on the `cc` command line. For example:

```
cc myprog.c -lm -lmalloc -o myprog
```

will search the math and malloc libraries for functions to be included in the executable program `myprog`.

Each entry in this section provides the function's name, identifies the library in which the function is located, describes the calling interface, and briefly describes the function's processing.

ANSI C syntax is used to describe function calls, although most UNIX compilers do not yet support the ANSI standard. This will rarely be a problem for programmers who must use a Kernighan and Ritchie compiler; full function prototypes are not required by these compilers, and ANSI C compilers will include the necessary function prototypes in standard header files.

UNIX System V has been ported to many different hardware environments. Although these versions of System V comply closely with the System V Interface Definition (SVID), differences in hardware inevitably force some deviation from the official release. For precise information when you use hardware-dependent functions, be sure to consult your system documentation.

_exit

S

```
void _exit (int status);
```

`_exit` exits the current process. The eight low-order bits of *status* are returned to the parent process.

If the parent process is not executing a wait, the calling process remains in the process table until the status is retrieved. Unless the parent process has set signal action to SIG_DFL or SIG_IGN, SIGCLD is posted to the parent process.

Warning

Open files are not closed; loss of data may result.

Related functions

`exit, shmat, wait`

_tolower

```
int _tolower (int c);
```

The argument *c* is assumed to be an uppercase letter. The corresponding lowercase letter is returned.

Warning

An unpredictable value will be returned if *c* is not the ASCII code for an uppercase letter.

Related functions

`_toupper, tolower, toupper`

_toupper

```
int _toupper (int c);
```

The argument *c* is assumed to be a lowercase letter. The corresponding uppercase letter is returned.

Warning

An unpredictable value will be returned if *c* is not the ASCII code for a lowercase letter.

Related functions

`_tolower, tolower, toupper`

abort

```
int abort (void);
```

An attempt is made to close all open files. A signal is generated that causes process termination with a dump.

Warning

If process catches or ignores the signal, `abort` will not behave as intended.

Related functions

`_exit, exit, signal`

abs

```
int abs (int i);
```

Returns

the absolute value of *i*

Warning

Machine implementation may not be able to represent the absolute value of maximum negative integer.

access

errno S

```
int access (const char *path, int
    amode);
```

Headers

`unistd.h`

The return value indicates whether the real user is permitted to access *path* as indicated by *amode*; *amode* must be zero or a combination of the bit values shown in table 4.

Table 4. Mode flags for access( )

Defined bit mask	Tests for
R_OK 04	Read permission
W_OK 02	Write permission
X_OK 01	Execute (search) permission
F_OK 00	Existence of file

Returns

0 if access permitted; –1 otherwise

Warning

The real user-ID is used to determine accessibility.

Related functions

```
chmod, exec, stat, setuid
```

acos

errno -lm

```
double acos (double x);
```

Headers

```
math.h
```

Returns

```
arccos(x)
```

alarm

S

```
unsigned alarm (unsigned sec);
```

The signal SIGALRM is scheduled to occur *sec* real seconds from now. Any previously scheduled alarm signal is cancelled. If the value of *sec* is zero, the only effect is to cancel any outstanding alarm.

Returns

the seconds remaining in a previously scheduled interval; if none exists, returns 0.

Warning

1. If not caught or ignored, SIGALRM will cause abnormal termination of the process.
2. Depending on the amount of other system activity, the signal may occur an indeterminate amount of time later than requested.

Related functions

```
pause, signal
```

asctime

```
char *asctime (struct tm *time);
```

Headers

`time.h`

`Asctime` converts values contained in `tm` structure pointed to by *time* to a character string suitable for display. The result string is

```
Sun Dec 17 09:19:13 1989\n\0
```

Returns

a pointer to a static character array containing the result

Related functions

`ctime, gmtime, localtime, time, time.h`

asin

errno -lm

```
double asin (double x);
```

Headers

`math.h`

Returns

arcsin(*x*)

assert

```
assert (expression)
```

Headers

`assert.h`

Calculates value of *expression*; if the result is non-zero, nothing happens. Otherwise, a diagnostic message is written to the standard-error file and the program is aborted (see `abort`).

`Assert` is a macro. To suppress generation of `assert` statements, specify the `cc` option `-DNDEBUG`.

atan

errno -lm

```
double atan (double x);
```

Headers

`math.h`

Returns

arctan(*x*)

atan2

errno -lm

```
double atan2 (double x, double y);
```

Headers

`math.h`

Returns

arctan(*x*/*y*). The result lies in the range of negative to positive pi radians.

atof

errno

```
double atof (const char *string);
```

Returns

the double-precision number represented by *string*. *String* may contain leading spaces, an optional sign character, one or more digits (decimal point is optional), and an optional exponent (an *e* or *E*, an optional sign character, and one or more digits).

Warning

If an over- or underflow would occur, HUGE or zero is returned and *errno* is set to EDOM.

Related functions

`atof, scanf, strtol`

atoi

```
int atoi (const char *string);
```

Returns

the integer value represented by *string*. *String* may contain leading spaces, an optional sign character, and one or more digits. `Atoi` is equivalent to

```
(int) strtol(string, (char**)0, 10)
```

Related functions

`atol, scanf, strtod, strtol`

atol

```
long atol (const char *string);
```

Returns

the long integer value represented by *string*. *String* may contain leading spaces, an optional sign character, and one or more digits.

Related functions

atoi, scanf, strtod, strtol

bsearch

```
void *bsearch (const void *key,
    const void *table, unsigned nel,
    unsigned width, int (*compar)());
```

Headers

search.h

Bsearch performs a binary search of the array pointed to by *table* for an entry matching *key*. Table is assumed to contain *nel* elements of *width* bytes each.

Compar is a user function with the assumed declaration:

```
int compar (const void *entry1,
 const void *entry2);
```

When *entry1* is equal to, greater than, or less than *entry2*, *compar* must return a zero, positive, or negative integer value, respectively.

Returns

a pointer to the table entry with a key value matching the *key* argument; NULL, if no such entry exists.

Related functions

hsearch, lsearch, tsearch, strcmp

calloc

errno

```
void *calloc (unsigned nelem, size_t
    size);
```

Headers

malloc.h

Returns

a pointer to an area of storage large enough to contain an array of *nelem* elements, each *size* bytes long. The area, properly aligned for any use, is initialized to binary zero. If an area of the requested size cannot be allocated, returns NULL. Because `calloc` uses `malloc` to allocate storage, `mallopt` has the expected effect.

Warning

The result of accessing storage outside the boundaries of the allocated array may cause abnormal termination.

Related functions

free, malloc, mallopt, realloc

ceil

-lm

```
double ceil (double x);
```

Headers

math.h

Returns

the smallest integer not less than *x*

Warning

`ceil(2.7)` returns 3, but `ceil(-2.7)` returns –2.

chdir

errno S

```
int chdir (const char *path);
```

The current working directory is set to *path*. The directory named by *path* must exist and must be readable by the effective user.

Returns

0 if successful; –1 otherwise

chmod

errno S

```
int chmod (const char *path, int
    mode);
```

Access permissions of the file named by *path* are set to the 12 low-order bits of *mode* (see table 5). Effective user must be super-user or the owner of the file.

Table 5. Chmod mode flags

Flag bit	Meaning
04000	Set-user-ID flag
02000	Set-group-ID flag
01000	Save-text-image flag
00400	Allow read by owner
00200	Allow write by owner
00100	Allow execute (search) by owner
00070	Allow read, write, or search by group
00007	Allow read, write, or search by others

To set the set-group-ID flag, the effective group-ID must be equal to the group-ID of the file. To set the save-text-image flag, the effective user-ID must be super-user.

Returns

0 if successful; –1 if file-access permissions could not be changed

Warning

The set-user-ID, set-group-ID, and save-text-image flags have no effect for a shell script or data file.

Related functions

chown, mknod

chown

errno S

```
int chown (const char *path, int
    owner, int group);
```

Owner- and group-ID of the file named by *path* are set to the numeric values of *owner* and *group*, respectively. Effective user-ID must be either super-user or the file owner.

The set-user-ID and set-group-ID flags are reset to zero unless `chown` is invoked by the super-user.

Returns

0 if successful; –1 otherwise

Related functions

chmod

clearerr

```
void clearerr (FILE *stream);
```

Headers

stdio.h

Any error or end-of-file flags in the FILE block pointed to by *stream* are reset, allowing normal stream-file I/O to continue.

When stream-file I/O functions detect an error or end-of-file condition, further I/O to the file is inhibited until the indication is reset.

Warning

`Clearerr` is implemented as a macro.

Related functions

`feof, ferror, fopen`

clock

```
time_t clock
```

Headers

`sys/types.h`

Returns time elapsed since previous call to `clock` as a number of microseconds. Accumulated time wraps after 2,147 seconds (35+ minutes).

Warning

Resolution of clock may be greater than 1 microsecond.

close

errno S

```
int close (int handle);
```

The file corresponding to *handle* is closed. All locks that may be held on the file (see `open`) are released. The file descriptor corresponding to *handle* is made available for reuse.

Returns

0 if successful; –1 otherwise

Warning

Use this function only for files opened with `open`, `creat`, `dup`, or `pipe`.

Related functions

`creat, exec, fclose, open, pipe`

closedir

errno R3

```
void closedir (DIR *dirp);
```

Headers

`sys/types.h, dirent.h`

The directory file pointed to by *dirp* is closed and all `malloc` storage is released.

Related functions

`dirent.h, opendir, readdir, rewinddir, seekdir, telldir`

cos

errno -lm

```
double cos (double x);
```

Headers

`math.h`

Returns

trigonometric cosine of argument *x* in radians

cosh

errno -lm

```
double cosh (double x);
```

Headers

`math.h`

Returns

hyperbolic cosine of *x*

creat

errno S

```
int creat (const char *path, int
    mode);
```

If the file named by *path* does not exist, it is created with access permissions equal to the nine low-order bits of *mode* as modified by the process file-creation mask (see `chmod` and `umask`). If the file exists, it is truncated to zero length. The file is then opened for writing (even if *mode* does not allow writing).

Effective user-ID must be super-user or have write permission.

`Creat` cannot create a directory, pipe, or special file.

Returns

handle of open file; –1 if unsuccessful

Related functions

`chmod, fopen, mknod, open, pipe, umask`

ctermid

```
char *ctermid (char *buf);
```

Headers

`stdio.h`

`Ctermid` returns the pathname of the terminal. If *buf* is not NULL, the pathname is stored in the character array pointed to by *buf*. The character array must be at least `L_ctermid` bytes long (defined in `stdio.h`).

Returns

value of *buf* (if *buf* is not NULL) or a pointer to a static character array containing the result.

Warning

`Ctermid` always returns the pathname `/dev/tty`.

Related functions

`ttyname`

ctime

```
char *ctime (time_t *clock);
```

Headers

`sys/types.h, time.h`

`Ctime` converts the value pointed to by *clock* to a character string. The value expresses the number of seconds elapsed since midnight January 1, 1970. The string format is

```
Sun Dec 17 09:19:13 1989\n\0
```

Returns

a pointer to an internal array containing the result

Related functions

`asctime, gmtime, localtime, time`

cuserid

```
char *cuserid (char *buf);
```

Headers

`stdio.h`

`Cuserid` returns the login name of the current user. *Buf* is either NULL or a pointer to a user-supplied character array at least `L_cuserid` bytes long where the name will be stored. (`L_cuserid` is defined in `stdio.h`.)

If the calling process was created by `/bin/login` or is a child of such a process, the returned value is the user's login name; otherwise, the returned value is that returned by `getpwuid` for the caller's real user-ID.

Returns

buf (if *buf* is not NULL); otherwise, returns a pointer to a static array within `cuserid`. If no appropriate user name can be found, a NULL pointer is returned, and the array pointed to by *buf* (if *buf* is not NULL) is cleared.

Related functions

`getlogin, getpwuid, getuid, logname`

daylight

```
extern int daylight;
```

Headers

`time.h`

The global variable *daylight* contains TRUE when daylight saving time conversion should be applied to obtain the current local time; zero, otherwise.

Warning

The vagaries of start and stop times for daylight saving time are such that indication of the *daylight* variable is probably wrong at certain times of year.

Related functions

`time, timezone, tzname, tzset`

drand48

```
double drand48 (void);
```

`Drand48` returns a double-precision pseudo-random number in the range 0-1.

Before the first call, the generator should be seeded using `srand48`, `seed48`, or `lcong48`.

Warning

If the same seed is used on each program execution, or if no seed is introduced, the same series of numbers will always be generated.

Related functions

`erand48, jrand48, lcong48, lrand48, mrand48, nrand48, rand, seed48, srand48`

dup

errno S

```
int dup (int handle);
```

The open file descriptor corresponding to *handle* is copied to the first unused file descriptor slot, and the handle of the copy is returned. Both file descriptors share the same file pointer; a read or write using either file descriptor changes current position of the file for both file descriptors.

`Dup` is used primarily to change assignment of standard input, standard output, and standard error files using a sequence similar to the following:

```
fd = open(path, O_WRONLY);
close(1);
dup(fd);
close(fd);
```

Returns

handle of new file descriptor; –1 if unsuccessful

Warning

When using `dup` to reassign a specific file descriptor, take care to ensure that all lower-numbered file descriptors are open.

Related functions

`close, exec, fcntl, open, pipe`

ecvt

```
char *ecvt (double num, int prec, int
    *exp, int *sign);
```

The value of *num* is converted to an equivalent base-10 representation as a string of *prec* digits. Leading zeroes are not stored; the last digit is rounded.

The radix point is assumed at the left of the first digit; the integer pointed to by *exp* is set to the number of bytes by which the radix point should be shifted left (negative values) or right (positive values) to obtain the true value of the number. The integer pointed to by *sign* is set to zero if *num* is zero or positive, or to –1 if *num* is negative.

Returns

a pointer to a static array containing the result

Warning

The static array is reused on each call.

Related functions

`fcvt, gcvt, printf`

edata

```
extern edata;
```

The address of `edata` (`&edata`) points to the first memory location beyond the initialized-data portion of the data segment. Systems not employing a segmented memory model may define the address of `edata` identically with that of `end`.

This variable is automatically defined by the compiler.

Warning

Attempts to reference `edata` may result in abnormal termination.

Related functions

`end, etext`

endpwent

```
void endpwent (void);
void endspent (void);
```

Password file used by `getpwent` or shadow file used by `getspent` is closed. `Endpwent` recovers resources allocated by `getpwent`, `getpwuid`, and `getpwnam`. `Endspent` recovers resources allocated by `getspent` and `getspnam` (*R3 only*).

Related functions

`getpwent, setpwent`

environ

```
extern char *environ[];
```

A global variable automatically defined by the compiler, `environ` points to an array of string pointers terminated with a NULL pointer; each element points to one of the `name=value` strings in the environment.

Related functions

`execle, getenv, putenv`

erand48

```
double erand48 (unsigned short
    lvalue[3]);
```

`Erand48` returns a double-precision pseudo-random number in the range 0–1.

The array pointed to by *lvalue* must contain a 48-bit value prior to invocation; upon return, it contains a new *X*-value that will be used to generate the next random number. This generator requires no seeding function.

Multiple independent random-number series can be generated by using `erand48`; maintain a separate *lvalue* array for each series.

Related functions

`drand48, jrand48, lrand48, mrand48, nrand48, rand`

erf

-lm

```
double erf (double x);
```

Headers

`math.h`

Returns

the value of the error function for *x*

erfc

-lm

```
double erfc (double x);
```

Headers

`math.h`

`Erfc` computes the complement of the error function (`1.0 - erf(x)`, for example). Use `erfc` to avoid loss of significance when *erf*(*x*) is a very small value.

errno

```
extern int errno;
```

Headers

`errno.h`

Errno is set by all system calls and most library functions when an error occurs. Its value, a code describing the error, may be used as an index into the `sys_errlist` array of message strings.

`Errno.h` defines names for most error codes.

Warning

The value of `errno` is not meaningful unless a function error was indicated, usually by a return value of –1.

Related functions

`sys_errlist, sys_nerr, perror`

etext

```
extern void etext();
```

`Etext` is not a usable function; its address (`&etext`) points to the first memory location beyond the program's code segment. Systems not employing code and data segments may define the address of `etext` identically with that of `end`.

`Etext` is automatically defined by the compiler.

Warning

Attempts to invoke `etext` may result in abnormal termination.

Related functions

`edata, end`

exec

errno S

```
int execl (char *path, char *arg0, ...
    , (char *)0);
int execle (char *path, char *arg0,
    ... , (char *)0, char *envp[]);
int execlp (char *file, char *arg0,
    ... , (char *)0);
int execv (char *path, char *argv[]);
int execve (char *path, char *argv[],
    char *envp[]);
int execvp (char *file, char *argv[]);
```

The program file named by *path* is loaded into memory and executed, replacing the calling program. No new process is created. Open files remain open, except those for which the close-on-exec flag has been set (see `fcntl`). Signal actions for which the action is *function address* are set to SIG_DFL (see `signal`).

If the access permissions of the executable file include the set-user-ID flag, the effective user-ID of the process is set to the file's owner-ID; the set-group-ID flag has a corresponding effect.

For `execlp` and `execvp`, directories in the PATH environment are searched for the named *file*.

Arguments *arg0, . . .* must be pointers to character strings and must be followed by a NULL pointer. Argument strings are copied into the new address space and passed to the called program.

Argy must point to an array of pointers to character strings; the last array element must be a NULL pointer. The strings are copied into the new address space and become the argument list for the new program.

Envp must be an array of pointers to character strings. The last pointer must be NULL. Each string must be an expression of the form *varname=value*.

If `exec` fails, control returns to the caller and *errno* indicates the reason.

Returns

–1 if unsuccessful; otherwise, does not return

Warning

Argument and environment strings must be saved in a system buffer while the new process address space is being created; the total number of bytes available may be as little as 5,120. Long argument lists should be avoided whenever possible.

Related functions

`chmod, execle, execlp, execv, execve, execvp, fcntl`

exit

S

```
void exit (int status);
```

`Exit` terminates the current process after performing cleanup actions, including the following:

- Closing all open files
- Detaching all attached shared-memory segments as if `shmdt` had been executed for each segment
- Adding the *semadj* value to each semaphore manipulated with the SEM_UNDO flag
- Removing all outstanding file locks

The eight low-order bits of *status* are made available to the parent process as a return value.

If parent process is not executing a `wait`, the calling process remains in the process table until its termination status is retrieved. SIGCLD is posted to the parent process unless the signal action is SIG_DFL or SIG_IGN.

Related functions

`_exit, fcntl, lock, semop, shmdt, wait`

exp

errno -lm

```
double exp (double x);
```

Headers

`math.h`

Returns

value of *e* (2.718...) raised to the power of *x*

Warning

Returns HUGE on overflow, or 0 on underflow, and sets *errno* to ERANGE.

fabs

-lm

```
double fabs (double x);
```

Headers

`math.h`

Returns

absolute value of *x*

fclose

errno

```
int fclose (FILE *stream);
```

Headers

`stdio.h`

The file pointed to by *stream* is closed. The contents of the stream buffer, if any, are written out. All storage allocated for the file is released.

Returns

0 if successful; –1 otherwise

Warning

Because the area pointed to by *stream* no longer exists, any subsequent reference using this pointer will have an unpredictable effect.

Related functions

`close, exit, fflush, fopen, setbuf`

fcntl

errno S

```
int fcntl (int handle, int command,
    int arg);
```

Headers

`fcntl.h`

`Fcntl` manipulates an open file in the manner specified by *command*. The file corresponding to *handle* must be open. For *command*, specify one of the following:

F_DUPFD: Copy file descriptor for *handle* to file descriptor slot that corresponds to *arg*, or to next higher unopen file descriptor. Handle of new copy is returned as value of the function.

F_GETFD: Return close-on-exec flag for file descriptor *handle*. Return value will be 0 (not set) or 1 (set).

F_SETFD: Set close-on-exec flag of file descriptor *handle* to value of *arg*. *Arg* must have value of 1 (set) or 0 (not set).

F_GETFL: Return file status flags as value of the function. Returned value will be value O_RDONLY, O_WRONLY, or O_RDWR, possibly combined with one or more of the values O_NDELAY, O_APPEND, and O_SYNC.

F_SETFL: Set file-status flags to value of *arg*. Only the O_NDELAY, O_APPEND, and O_SYNC flags may be set.

F_GETLK: The `flock` struct pointed to by *arg* will be changed to describe existing file lock that would prevent setting of lock described by the struct. If no conflict is found, struct is not changed except that lock type is set to F_UNLCK.

F_SETLK: File segment lock described by `flock` struct pointed to by *arg* will be set, if possible. If lock cannot be granted, –1 will be returned.

F_SETLKW: Same as F_SETLK, except that process is set to wait until lock can be granted.

The F_GETLK, F_SETLK, and F_SETLKW operations require *arg* to be a pointer to a `flock` struct declared in the `fcntl.h` header file. The struct contains at least the following members:

`l_type`: One of the values F_RDLCK, F_WRLCK, or F_UNLCK. A read lock (F_RDLCK) on a file segment prevents any other process from acquiring a write lock on any part of that segment, whereas a write lock (F_WRLCK) prevents any other lock on any part of that segment (exclusive use). The unlock type (F_UNLCK) releases existing lock held by caller.

`l_start`: The byte offset from start of file to first byte of file segment to be locked.

`l_len`: Number of bytes in file segment. If zero, segment extends to end of file, even if length of file later changes. If value of `l_start` is also zero, entire file is locked.

`l_pid`: Used only by F_GETLK to identify process that owns conflicting file lock.

Returns

–1 if unsuccessful; otherwise, as described in preceding paragraphs. Return value for F_SETFD, F_SETFL, F_GETLK, F_SETLK, and F_SETLKW is not defined.

Related functions

`close, exec, open`

fcvt

```
char *fcvt (double num, int prec, int
    *exp, int *sign);
```

The value of *num* is converted to an equivalent base-10 representation as a string of digits. The result string consists of the digits of the integer portion, followed immediately by *prec* fractional digits. Leading zeroes are not stored; the last digit is rounded.

The radix point is assumed to be to the left of the first digit; the integer pointed to by *exp* is set to the number of bytes by which the radix point should be shifted left (negative values) or right (positive values) to obtain the number's true value. Integer pointed to by *sign* is set to zero if *num* is zero or positive, to –1 if *num* is negative.

Returns

a pointer to a static array containing the result

Warning

The static array is reused on each call.

Related functions

`ecvt, gcvt, printf`

fdopen

errno

```
FILE *fdopen (int handle, const char
    *type);
```

Headers

`stdio.h`

Creates and initializes a FILE struct to support access of type *type* to the open file *handle*. For *type*, specify one of the values allowed by `fopen`.

Returns

pointer to new FILE block, if successful; NULL pointer, if unsuccessful

Related functions

`creat, dup, fopen, freopen, open, pipe`

feof

```
int feof (FILE *stream);
```

Headers

`stdio.h`

Returns

EOF if end-of-file has been detected previously for the file *stream*; otherwise, returns zero.

Note that once stream-file I/O functions detect end-of-file, the indication is preserved; further I/O operations for this file are inhibited until the indication is reset.

Warning

`Feof` is implemented as a macro.

Related functions

`clearerr, ferror, fopen`

ferror

```
int ferror (FILE *stream);
```

Headers

`stdio.h`

Returns

a non-zero value if any previous error has been detected for the file *stream*; otherwise, returns zero.

Note that once stream-file I/O functions detect an error indication, the indication is preserved and further I/O operations are inhibited until the indication is reset.

Warning

`Ferror` is implemented as a macro.

Related functions

`clearerr, feof, fopen`

fflush

errno

```
int fflush (FILE *stream);
```

Headers

`stdio.h`

Any output data currently buffered for stream file *stream* is written to the external file or device.

Returns

0 if successful; –1 otherwise

Related functions

`fclose, setbuf`

fgetc

```
int fgetc (FILE *stream);
```

Headers

`stdio.h`

Returns

the next character in the stream file *stream*, or a character inserted into the stream by a previous call to `ungetc`. The file pointer is advanced or the character inserted by `ungetc` is deleted, as appropriate.

EOF is returned at end of file or if an error occurs.

Related functions

`fclose, feof, ferror, fgets, fopen, fputc, fread, fseek, getc, gets, putc, puts, read, scanf, ungetc`

fgets

```
char *fgets (char *buffer, int size,
   FILE *stream);
```

Headers

`stdio.h`

`Fgets` reads characters from *stream* and stores them in the character array pointed to by *buffer* until a newline character is stored, *size* characters have been read, or end of file is reached. A null character is stored at the end of the input string.

Returns

a pointer to the stored string. If end of file occurs before any characters are stored, the NULL pointer is returned.

Warning

If the input line is longer than *size* characters, each call to `fgets` will return a *size*-byte segment of the line until the last segment has been read.

The `gets` and `fgets` functions handle newline character differently: `fgets` stores newline at the end of the input string; `gets` does not.

Related functions

`ferror, fopen, fputs, fread, getc, gets, scanf`

fileno

```
int fileno (FILE *stream);
```

Headers

`stdio.h`

Returns

the handle of the file descriptor on which the stream file *stream* is open

Warning

`Fileno` is implemented as a macro.

Related functions

`fopen, open`

floor

-lm

```
double floor (double x);
```

Headers

`math.h`

Returns

largest integer not greater than *x*

Warning

`Floor` differs from the integer part of *x* for negative numbers. For example, `floor(-2.7)` is –3.

fmod

-lm

```
double fmod (double x, double y);
```

Headers

`math.h`

Returns

x `mod` *y*

fopen

errno

```
int fopen (const char *path, const
    char *type);

extern FILE *stdin, *stdout, *stderr;
```

Headers

`stdio.h`

The file named by *path* is opened for operations of type *type*. A FILE block and stream buffer are allocated using `malloc`. The stream files *stdin*, *stdout*, and *stderr* are always open and may be used without an explicit `fopen` request.

Stream files buffer I/O to minimize the number of `read` and `write` calls to the kernel. The size of the buffer defaults to BUFSIZ defined in `stdio.h`, but may be overridden using `setbuf` and `setvbuf`.

Type may specify one of the following values:

"r" File is opened for reading. File pointer is set to first byte of file.

"w" File is opened for writing. File is created if it does not already exist; otherwise, it is truncated to zero length. File pointer set to first byte of file.

"a" File is opened for append. File is created if it does not already exist. File pointer set to end of file.

"r+" File is opened for both reading and writing; the file pointer is set to first byte of file. A `read` operation may not be followed by a `write` (nor a `write` by a `read`) unless an intervening `fseek` or `rewind` is performed. A `write` may immediately follow a `read` that returned end-of-file.

"w+" File is opened for update. If file does not exist, it is created; otherwise, file is truncated to zero length. Either reading or writing may be performed (with the restrictions noted previously for type "r+"). File pointer is set to first byte of file.

"a+" File is opened for update. If file does not exist, it is created; otherwise, its length remains unchanged. File pointer is set following last byte of file. Reading may be performed anywhere in file, using `fseek` or `rewind`, but all writes are forced to occur at end of file.

Note that when a file is open for append (either type "a" or "a+"), two or more processes may write simultaneously to the file without harm; their output will be interleaved but will not overlap.

Returns

a FILE pointer, if successful; otherwise, NULL pointer is returned and *errno* identifies the error.

Related functions

`clearerr, creat, fclose, fread, fseek, fwrite, rewind, setbuf, setvbuf, open`

fork

errno S

```
int fork (void)
```

`Fork` creates a new (child) process by making a copy of the current (parent) process. Both processes then continue execution of the same program.

Initially, the file descriptors of the child process are a copy of those of the parent process; open file descriptors share a common file pointer. The child process inherits all signal actions in effect for the parent process. The child does not inherit the file locks or *semadj* values of its parent.

The parent process will be notified of the termination of its child processes by receipt of the signal SIGCLD or by `wait` function.

Returns

–1 and fails if the limit on the total number of processes is exceeded; otherwise, zero is returned to child process, and child's process-ID is returned to parent process.

Related functions

`dup, exec, signal, wait`

fprintf

errno

```
int fprintf (FILE *stream, const char
    *format, ...);
```

Headers

`stdio.h`

`Fprintf` differs from `printf` in that `fprintf` writes to *stream* instead of to standard output.

Returns

the number of characters written to *stream*, or a negative number on error

Related functions

`printf, putc, puts, fscanf, sprintf, vfprintf`

fputc

```
int fputc (int c, FILE *stream);
```

Headers

`stdio.h`

`Fputc` is identical to `putc` except that `fputc` is a real function, not a macro.

Returns

the value *c*

Warning

Use `putc` whenever possible; `fputc` imposes more overhead than `putc` due to function entry and exit code.

Related functions

`putc`

fputs

errno

```
int fputs (const char *string, FILE
    *stream);
```

Headers

`stdio.h`

The string pointed to by *string* is written to *stream*. Neither a newline character nor the ending null character is written. `Fputs` behaves as though each character of *string* were written successively by `putc`.

Returns

EOF on error; otherwise, zero

Warning

The `puts` and `fputs` functions use opposite conventions for writing a trailing newline character to output.

Related functions

`ferror, fgets, fopen, putc, puts`

fread

errno

```
int fread (void *ptr, int size, int
    elems, FILE *stream);
```

Headers

`stdio.h`

`Fread` retrieves several data elements, each *size* bytes long, from the stream file *stream* and stores them in consecutive elements of the array pointed to by *ptr*. Reading stops when *elems* elements have been transferred, EOF is encountered, or an I/O error occurs. If *elems* is zero or negative, no elements are transferred. A maximum of 65,535 bytes can be transferred in a call.

Returns

the number of elements actually stored

Related functions

`fopen, fwrite, getc, gets, putc, read, scanf`

free

```
void free (void *area);
```

Headers

`malloc.h`

The storage pointed to by *area* is released and made available for subsequent reallocation.

Warning

Undefined results occur if the value of *area* is not a pointer previously returned by `malloc`, `calloc`, or `realloc`.

Related functions

`calloc, malloc, realloc`

freopen

errno

```
FILE *freopen (const char *path, const
    char *type, FILE *stream);
```

Headers

`stdio.h`

The file pointed to by *stream* is closed, then reopened for the file named by *path* for access *type*. (See `fopen` for the legal values of *type*.) If reopen fails, the FILE pointed to by *stream* will have been closed. `Freopen` is useful for changing the file to which the standard files *stdin*, *stdout*, and *stderr* are assigned.

Returns

the value of *stream* if successful; otherwise, NULL is returned and *errno* is set to indicate the error.

Related functions

`fclose, fdopen, fopen`

fscanf

errno

```
int fscanf (FILE *stream, const char
    *format, ...);
```

Headers

`stdio.h`

`Fscanf` is identical to `scanf` except that `fscanf` reads the stream file pointed to by *stream* instead of standard input.

Returns

number of values converted and stored; EOF, if end of file was encountered before any values were stored.

Related functions

`fclose, ferror, fopen, fread, getc, scanf, sscanf`

fseek

```
int fseek (FILE *stream, long offset,
   int origin);
```

Headers

`stdio.h`

A logical seek is performed for the stream file *stream* by setting an internal file pointer to a new byte offset value. Any end-of-file indication is cleared.

The new offset is computed as the sum of the signed value of *offset* and a displacement implied by the value of *origin*. Table 6 lists allowable values of *origin*.

Table 6. Origin values

Origin	Implied position in file
0	Beginning (offset=0)
1	Current position
2	End of file

Negative offsets may be used, provided that the resulting file offset is not negative.

Returns

a non-zero value if the seek cannot be performed; otherwise, zero.

Warning

Some types of files (terminals, communication lines and pipes) cannot be repositioned. `Fseek` is intended for use with standard disk files; other uses may not be portable. `Fseek` cancels the effect of any previous `ungetc`.

Related functions

`fopen, ftell, lseek, rewind`

fstat

errno S

```
int fstat (int handle, struct stat
    *buf);
```

Headers

sys/types.h sys/stat.h

`Fstat` returns information about the open file associated with *handle* in a user-provided structure pointed to by *buf*. Struct `stat` is defined in `stat.h`.

Returns

0 if successful; –1 otherwise

Related functions

`access, stat`

ftell

```
long ftell (FILE *stream);
```

Headers

`stdio.h`

Returns

the current position of the stream file *stream* as a byte offset from the beginning of the file

Warning

When *stream* is opened for a file type that does not support seek operations, the value returned by `ftell` is meaningless.

Related functions

`fopen, fseek`

ftw

```
int ftw (const char *path, int
    (*fn)(), int depth);
```

Headers

`ftw.h`

`Ftw` recursively descends a directory hierarchy, beginning with the directory named by *path*, calling *fn* for each file or directory encountered. When a directory is found, `ftw` opens a new file descriptor if the number of files already opened by `ftw` is less than *depth*; otherwise, `ftw` reuses an open file descriptor.

The declaration of *fn* is

```
int fn (char *filename, struct stat
  *statbuf, int flag);
```

where *filename* points to the name of the file or directory, *statbuf* points to a structure containing the output of `stat`, and *flag* is one of the following values:

FTW_F if *filename* is a file
FTW_D if *filename* is a directory
FTW_DNR if *filename* is a directory that cannot be read
FTW_NS if `stat` failed

When traversal is complete or the user function returns a non-zero value, `ftw` closes all files it opened, releases all storage obtained by calls to `malloc`, and returns.

Returns

last value returned by user function *fn*

Warning

`Ftw` can run out of free storage when traversing a very deep directory structure. `Ftw` will run faster if the value of *depth* is at least as large as the deepest nesting level in the directory tree to be traversed.

Related functions

`dir.h, opendir, stat, malloc`

fwrite

errno

```
int fwrite (const void *ptr, int size,
    int elems, FILE *stream);
```

Headers

`stdio.h`

`Fwrite` writes successive elements of the array *ptr* (each *size* bytes in length) to the file *stream*. Writing stops after *elems* elements or when an I/O error occurs. If *elems* is zero or negative, no elements are transferred. A maximum of 65,535 bytes can be transferred in a call.

Returns

the number of array elements actually written

Related functions

`fopen, fread, printf, putc, write`

gamma

errno -lm

```
double gamma (double x);
```

Headers

`math.h, values.h`

Returns

natural logarithm of absolute value of gamma function at *x*. The sign of the function at *x* is stored in the integer variable *signgam*. The actual gamma function can be computed as the product of *signgam* and `exp(g)`, when `g` is not larger than LN_MAXDOUBLE as defined in `values.h`.

gcvt

```
char *gcvt (double num, int prec, char
    *buf);
```

The base-10 representation of *num*, rounded to *prec* digits, is stored in the character array pointed to by *buf*. The result contains a decimal point at the proper position, and a sign, if necessary.

An attempt is made to store the result in fixed-point notation; if unsuccessful, the result will be stored in exponential notation.

Returns

pointer value of *buf*

Related functions

`ecvt, fcvt, printf`

getc

```
int getc (FILE *stream);
```

getcwd

errno

```
char *getcwd (char *buf, int size);
```

The pathname of the current directory is stored in the array pointed to by *buf*; length of pathname stored will not exceed *size* bytes.

If *buf* is NULL, a storage area *size* bytes in length is allocated to hold the pathname.

Returns

NULL if storage cannot be acquired by `malloc`, or if the *size* is less than the length of the pathname of the current directory. Otherwise, a pointer to the pathname string is returned.

Warning

The pathname of the current directory is determined by reading the piped output of `pwd`; this entails significant overhead.

getegid

S

```
unsigned short getegid (void);
```

Returns

the effective group-ID of the calling process

Related functions

`execl, getgid, getuid`

getenv

```
char *getenv (const char *name);
```

`Getenv` searches the environment for a string of the format `name=value` for a matching occurrence of *name*.

Returns

a pointer to the string following the = in environment variable; if a match is not found, returns NULL.

Related functions

`putenv`

geteuid

S

```
unsigned short geteuid (void);
```

Returns

the effective user-ID of the calling process

Related functions

`execl, getgid, getuid, setuid`

getgid

S

```
unsigned short getgid (void);
```

Returns

the real group-ID of the calling process

Related functions

`getuid, getegid, setgid`

getlogin

```
char *getlogin (void);
```

Returns

a pointer to the current user's login name, as found in `/etc/utmp`. NULL is returned if the login name cannot be identified.

Warning

The result string is stored in a static character array that is reused on each call.

Related functions

`cuserid, getpwuid, getuid, logname`

getopt

```
int getopt (int argc, const char
   *argv[], const char *flags);
extern char *optarg;
extern int optind, opterr;
```

`Getopt` parses option flags in the argument list *argv*, returning each keyletter found, together with any value string that may be present. Each call to `getopt` returns the next option keyletter in the argument list.

The *flags* string defines the legal keyletters. If a keyletter is expected to have an accompanying value string, the character **:** must follow that keyletter.

A keyletter with an accompanying value string must be the last keyletter in a group of flags; all remaining characters in the argument are assumed to be the value string for the keyletter.

Optarg points to the value string accompanying the keyletter.

Optind always indicates the index of the next unprocessed argument in the argument list. Its value can be used after `getopt` has returned to locate remaining arguments.

Opterr is a boolean flag. If 1, `getopt` will generate error messages; if 0, `getopt` will not write error messages. In either case, an ASCII value of '?' is returned for an illegal option keyletter. *Opterr* is initialized to 1.

Returns

the next option keyletter in the argument list as an integer ASCII code; if an illegal keyletter is found, '?' is returned; if no more keyletters are found, returns EOF.

getpass

```
char *getpass (const char *prompt);
```

The string pointed to by *prompt* is written to `/dev/tty`, then input is read with echoing disabled up to the next newline or end of file. All but the first eight characters of typed input is discarded.

Returns

pointer to typed input string; NULL, on error.

Warning

Input is stored in a static array that is reused on each call.

Related functions

`crypt`

getpgrp

S

```
int getpgrp (void);
```

Returns

process group-ID of calling process. Processes sharing the same terminal are members of same process group.

Related functions

`fork, getpid, getppid`

getpid

S

```
int getpid (void);
```

Returns

process-ID of the current process.

Related functions

`fork, getpgrp, getppid`

getppid

S

```
int getppid (void);
```

Returns

process ID of the parent process.

Related functions

`fork, getpid`

getpwent

```
struct passwd *getpwent (void);
struct spwd *getspent (void);
```

Headers

`pwd.h shadow.h`

On the first call to `getpwent`, the password file `/etc/passwd` is opened and the first line of the file is stored in an internal structure, the address of which is returned to the caller. Successive calls to `getpwent` will retrieve (in turn) each line of `/etc/passwd` file.

`Passwd` struct is described in `pwd.h` header file.

`Getspent` performs equivalent services for the shadow file (*R3 only*).

Returns

a pointer to an internal static `passwd` structure (`spwd` structure if `getspent`); NULL, if no more entries exist in the file.

Related functions

`endpwent, fgetpwent, getpwent, getpwnam, getpwuid, pwd.h, setpwent, shadow.h`

getpwnam

```
struct passwd *getpwnam (const char
    *name);
struct spwd *getspnam (const char
    *name);
```

Headers

`pwd.h, shadow.h`

Returns

a pointer to an internal static `passwd` structure; NULL if the specified login name does not occur in `/etc/passwd`. The struct displays the line of `/etc/passwd` that defines *name*.

`Pwd.h` file declares the `passwd` structure.

`Getspnam` performs the equivalent function for the shadow file (/etc/shadow). (*R3 only*)

Warning

`Getpwnam` calls `getpwent` to scan the `/etc/passwd` file. If `endpwent` is not called, the file will remain open, reducing the number of file descriptors available for application use.

Related functions

`endpwent, fgetpwent, getpwent, getpwnam, pwd.h, setpwent, shadow.h`

getpwuid

```
struct passwd *getpwuid (int user_id);
```

Headers

`pwd.h`

Returns

a pointer to an internal static `passwd` structure; NULL, if *user-id* does not occur in the `/etc/passwd` file. The struct displays the line of `/etc/passwd` that defines *user_id*.

`Pwd.h` contains a description of struct `passwd`.

Warning

`Getpwuid` calls `getpwent` to scan the `/etc/passwd` file. If `endpwent` is not called, the file will remain open, reducing the number of file descriptors available for application use.

Related functions

`endpwent, fgetpwent, getpwent, getpwnam, pwd.h, setpwent`

gets

```
char *gets (char *buffer);
```

Headers

`stdio.h`

`Gets` reads characters from the standard-input file `stdin` and stores them in the character array pointed to by *buffer* until a newline character is read or end of file is reached. The newline character is not stored. A null character is stored at the end of the string.

Returns

a pointer to the stored string. If end of file occurs before any characters are stored, NULL is returned.

Warning

The `gets` function is dangerous; it will attempt to store an indefinite number of characters in the array pointed to by *buffer*, possibly overrunning its end. Use `fgets` instead.

Related functions

`ferror, fgets, fopen, fread, getc, puts, scanf`

getuid

S

```
unsigned short getuid (void);
```

Returns

real user-ID of the calling process.

Related functions

`geteuid, getgid, setuid`

getw

```
int getw (FILE *stream);
```

Headers

stdio.h

Returns

the next integer taken from the stream file *stream*. Number of bytes read is equal to size of an integer. No alignment of the file pointer is forced or assumed. EOF is returned at end of file.

Warning

Since all legal values of an integer can be returned by `getw`, end of file should be checked with `feof`. The use of `getw` is not portable.

Related functions

feof, fopen, fread, fseek, getc, scanf

gmtime

```
struct tm *gmtime (time_t *clock);
```

Headers

time.h

`Gmtime` converts time-of-day value pointed to by *clock* to a `tm` structure. Values returned are for the GMT time zone.

Returns

a pointer to a static `tm` structure in `gmtime`

Related functions

asctime, ctime, localtime, time, time.h

hcreate

```
int hcreate (int n);
```

`Hcreate` creates a new hash search table with enough space to hold *n* entries. The table is initially empty.

`Hcreate` must be invoked before `hsearch`. Only one hash table can be used at a time.

Returns

zero if insufficient memory is available; otherwise, a non-zero value.

Related functions

`hdestroy, hsearch`

hdestroy

```
void hdestroy (void);
```

Use `hdestroy` to delete an existing hash table; all storage dedicated to the table is released. A new table can be created with `hcreate` after `hdestroy` has been executed.

Related functions

`hcreate, hsearch`

hsearch

```
void *hsearch (ENTRY item, int
   action);
```

Headers

`search.h`

`Hsearch` searches a hash table for an entry containing a specified key value. *Item.key* points to the key value to be found. *Action* specifies the action to be taken if the key value is *not* found in the table: ENTER causes the *item* to be added to the table; FIND suppresses the insertion of *item*.

Returns

a pointer to a struct of type ENTRY having a key value matching that of *item*; or a pointer to a new table entry, if *item* was not found in the table and the value of *action* was ENTER; or NULL, if *item* was not found and the value of *action* was FIND.

Related functions

`hcreate, hdestroy, search.h`

hypot

errno -lm

```
double hypot (double x, double y);
```

Headers

`math.h`

Returns

`sqrt(x*x + y*y)` computed in a manner to avoid spurious overflow or underflow.

ioctl

errno S

```
int ioctl (int handle, int request,
    ...);
```

`Ioctl` performs device-specific functions for character-special devices. (Refer to section 7 of the System V documentation for specific information).

Returns

–1 if an error occurs; otherwise, value returned depends on request.

Warning

Valid request types and their meaning vary between implementations of System V. In general, programs using `ioctl` are not portable across implementations, releases, or versions of UNIX.

Related functions

`fcntl`

isalnum

```
int isalnum (int character);
```

Headers

`ctype.h`

`Isalnum` tests whether *character* is an uppercase letter, a lowercase letter, or a decimal digit (0-9).

Returns

1 if TRUE; 0 if FALSE

Warning

A meaningless result will be returned if *character* is outside the range of valid ASCII codes (0-127).

Related functions

`isalpha, isascii, iscntrl, isdigit, isgraph, islower, isprint, ispunct, isspace, isupper, isxdigit`

isalpha

```
int isalpha (int character);
```

Headers

`ctype.h`

`Isalpha` tests if *character* is a letter (a-z or A-Z).

Returns

non-zero value if true; otherwise, zero.

Warning

A meaningless result value will be returned if *character* is outside the range of valid ASCII codes (0-127).

Related functions

`isalnum, isascii, iscntrl, isdigit, isgraph, islower, isprint, ispunct, isspace, isupper, isxdigit`

isascii

```
int isascii (int character);
```

Headers

`ctype.h`

`Isascii` tests whether *character* is a valid ASCII code. Defined for all possible values of *character*.

Returns

1 if TRUE; 0 if FALSE

Related functions

`isalnum, isalpha, iscntrl, isdigit, isgraph, islower, isprint, ispunct, isspace, isupper, isxdigit`

isatty

```
int isatty (int handle);
```

Returns

1 if the device corresponding to *handle* is a terminal; otherwise, 0.

Related functions

`ctermid, ttyname`

iscntrl

```
int iscntrl (int character);
```

Headers

`ctype.h`

`Iscntrl` tests whether *character* is a control character (less than 040 or equal to 0177).

Returns

1 if TRUE; 0 if FALSE

Warning

A meaningless result will be returned if *character* is outside the range of valid ASCII codes (0-127).

Related functions

`isalnum, isalpha, isascii, isdigit, isgraph, islower, isprint, ispunct, isspace, isupper, isxdigit`

isdigit

```
int isdigit (int character);
```

Headers

`ctype.h`

`Isdigit` tests whether *character* is a decimal digit.

Returns

1 if TRUE; 0 if FALSE

Warning

A meaningless result value will be returned if *character* is outside the range of valid ASCII codes (0-127).

Related functions

`isalnum, isalpha, isascii, iscntrl, isgraph, islower, isprint, ispunct, isspace, isupper, isxdigit`

isgraph

```
int isgraph (int character);
```

Headers

`ctype.h`

`Isgraph` tests whether *character* is a printable character other than a blank.

Returns

1 if TRUE; 0 if FALSE

Warning

A meaningless result value will be returned if *character* is outside the range of valid ASCII codes (0-127).

Related functions

`isalnum, isalpha, isascii, iscntrl, isdigit, islower, isprint, ispunct, isspace, isupper, isxdigit`

islower

```
int islower (int character);
```

Headers

`ctype.h`

`Islower` tests whether *character* is lowercase (a-z).

Returns

1 if TRUE; 0 if FALSE.

Warning

A meaningless result value will be returned if *character* is outside the range of valid ASCII codes (0-127).

Related functions

`isalnum, isalpha, isascii, iscntrl, isdigit, isgraph, isprint, ispunct, isspace, isupper, isxdigit`

isprint

```
int isprint (int character);
```

Headers

`ctype.h`

`Isprint` tests whether *character* is a printable character, including a blank.

Returns

1 if TRUE; 0 if FALSE.

Warning

A meaningless result value will be returned if *character* is outside the range of valid ASCII codes (0-127).

Related functions

`isalnum, isalpha, isascii, iscntrl, isdigit, isgraph, islower, ispunct, isspace, isupper, isxdigit`

ispunct

```
int ispunct (int character);
```

Headers

`ctype.h`

`Ispunct` tests whether *character* is a punctuation mark.

Returns

1 if TRUE; 0 if FALSE.

Warning

A meaningless result value will be returned if *character* is outside the range of valid ASCII codes (0-127).

Related functions

`isalnum, isalpha, isascii, iscntrl, isdigit, isgraph, islower, isprint, isspace, isupper, isxdigit`

isspace

```
int isspace (int character);
```

Headers

`ctype.h`

`Isspace` tests whether *character* is a space, tab, new-line, carriage return, vertical tab, or form feed.

Returns

1 if TRUE; 0 if FALSE

Warning

A meaningless result value will be returned if *character* is outside the range of valid ASCII codes (0-127).

Related functions

`isalnum, isalpha, isascii, iscntrl, isdigit, isgraph, islower, isprint, ispunct, isupper, isxdigit`

isupper

```
int isupper (int character);
```

Headers

`ctype.h`

`Isupper` tests whether *character* is uppercase (A-Z).

Returns

1 if TRUE; 0 if FALSE

Warning

A meaningless result value will be returned if *character* is outside the range of valid ASCII codes (0-127).

Related functions

`isalnum, isalpha, isascii, iscntrl, isdigit, isgraph, islower, isprint, ispunct, isspace, isxdigit`

isxdigit

```
int isxdigit (int character);
```

Headers

`ctype.h`

`Isxdigit` tests whether *character* is a hexadecimal digit (0-9, a-f, or A-F).

Returns

1 if TRUE; 0 if FALSE

Warning

A meaningless result value will be returned if *character* is outside the range of valid ASCII codes (0-127).

Related functions

isalnum, isalpha, isascii, iscntrl, isdigit, isgraph, islower, isprint, ispunct, isspace, isupper

j0

errno -lm

```
double j0 (double x);
```

Headers

math.h

Returns

Bessel function of the first kind, of order 0, for argument *x*. The function is defined for positive values of *x* less than some large value; other values cause a *matherr* condition to be recognized.

j1

errno -lm

```
double j1 (double x);
```

Headers

math.h

Returns

Bessel function of the first kind, of order 1, for argument *x*. The function is defined for positive values of *x* less than some large value; other values cause a *matherr* condition to be recognized.

jn

errno -lm

```
double jn (double x);
```

Headers

math.h

Returns

Bessel function of the first kind, of order n, for argument *x*. The function is defined for positive values of *x* less than some large value; other values cause a *matherr* condition to be recognized.

jrand48

```
long jrand48 (unsigned short
   lvalue[3]);
```

`Jrand48` returns a pseudo-random number uniformly distributed over the range –2,147,483,648 to 2,147,483,647.

The array pointed to by *lvalue* must contain a 48-bit value prior to invocation; upon return, it contains the *X*-value that will be used to generate the next random number. No seeding function is required.

Using `jrand48`, multiple independent random-number series can be generated by maintaining a separate *lvalue* array for each series.

Related functions

`drand48, erand48, lrand48, mrand48, nrand48, rand`

kill

errno S

```
int kill (int pid, int sig);
```

Headers

signal.h

`Kill` sends the signal *sig* to the process or group of processes implied by *pid*.

Sig must be one of the signals defined for `signal`, or zero. If zero, no signal is actually sent but all other error checking is performed.

Pid may be one of the following:

- *-n* *Sig* is sent to all processes in process group *n*.
- -1 *Sig* is sent to all processes having a real user-ID equal to the effective user-ID of the calling process; if the effective user is super-user, the signal is sent to all processes.
- 0 *Sig* is sent to all processes in the caller's process group.
- *n* *Sig* is sent to process *n*.

Returns

0 if successful; –1 otherwise.

Warning

The effect of `kill` is determined by the signal action defined by the receiving process.

Related functions

`getpid, setpgrp, signal`

lcong48

```
void lcong48 (unsigned short
    initializers[7]);
```

`Lcong48` seeds the random-number-generating functions `drand48`, `lrand48`, and `mrand48`.

Initializers[0] through *initializers*[2] replace the 48-bit *X*-value of the generator; *initializers*[3] through *initializers*[5] replace the 48-bit multiplier; *initializers*[6] replaces the 16-bit addend.

Warning

A subsequent call to `seed48` or `srand48` will reset the multiplier and addend values of the algorithm to their default values.

Related functions

`drand48, erand48, jrand48, lrand48, mrand48, nrand48, rand, seed48, srand48`

lfind

```
void *lfind (const void *key, const
   void *table, unsigned

  nel, unsigned width, int
   (*compar)());
```

Headers

`search.h`

`Lfind` searches an unordered table of items; *key* points to the value to be found in the table, *table* points to the first element in the table, *nel* is the number of table entries, *width* is the length of an entry in bytes, and *compar* points to a user function declared as

```
int compar (const void *entry1,
 const void *entry2);
```

When *entry1* is equal to, greater than, or less than *entry2*, *compar* must return a zero, positive, or negative integer value, respectively.

Returns

a pointer to a table entry matching the *key* argument; NULL, if no such entry is found.

Related functions

`lsearch`

link

errno S

```
int link (const char *path1, const
   char *path2);
```

Path1 must name an existing file, and *path2* must not exist. A directory entry is created for *path2* so that the same file is referenced by both path names. The directory entry for *path2* must be made in the same file system as the file pointed to by *path1*; that is, a link may not cross file systems.

Returns

0 if successful; –1 otherwise.

Related functions

`unlink`

localtime

```
struct tm *localtime (time_t*clock);
```

Headers

`sys/types.h, time.h`

`Localtime` converts the value pointed to by *clock* to a `tm` structure using the local time zone.

Returns

a pointer to a static `tm` struct in `localtime`.

Related functions

`asctime, ctime, gmtime, time, time.h`

lockf

errno

```
int lockf (int handle, int function,
   long size);
```

Headers

`unistd.h`

`Lockf` provides an interface to the file-locking capabilities of `fcntl`. *Handle* must identify an open file descriptor. The file segment beginning at the current file position and extending forward or backward *size* bytes is locked, unlocked, or tested for conflicting locks according to the value of *function*. A *size* of zero means "through" end of file.

Both F_LOCK and F_TLOCK lock the file segment if no conflicting locks exist; otherwise, F_LOCK waits until the entire segment is available, whereas F_TLOCK returns –1 with *errno* set to EACCES. Adjacent and overlapping locks set by the same process are merged into a single locked segment. Nonexistent parts of the file may be locked.

F_ULOCK unlocks all locked segments included in the range specified by *size*. A segment may be partially unlocked.

F_TEST returns zero if no portion of the range overlaps a file segment locked by another process; otherwise, returns –1 and *errno* is set to EACCES.

Returns

zero if F_TEST found no conflicting lock, or if F_LOCK, F_TLOCK, or F_ULOCK was successful. Otherwise, sets *errno* and returns –1.

Warning

Future versions of System V may store EAGAIN instead of EACCES. Because file-locking is not compatible with stream files, avoid `fopen` and related functions when using `lockf`.

Related functions

`fcntl, lseek, open`

log

errno -lm

```
double log (double x);
```

Headers

math.h

Returns

ln(*x*) for positive *x*.

Warning

Returns -HUGE and sets *errno* to EDOM when *x* is zero or negative.

log10

errno -lm

```
double log10 (double x);
```

Headers

math.h

Returns

base-10 logarithm of *x* for positive *x*.

Warning

Returns -HUGE and sets *errno* to EDOM when *x* is zero or negative.

logname

-lPW

```
char *logname (void);
```

Returns

the value of the $LOGNAME environment variable.

Related functions

`cuserid, getpwuid`

longjmp

```
void longjmp (jmp_buf env, int code);
```

Headers

`setjmp.h`

Use `longjmp` to return to the function that last used `setjmp` to set the value of *env*. The value of *code* is used as the apparent return value of `setjmp`; if *code* is zero, it is forced to 1 so that a `longjmp` return can be distinguished from a normal `setjmp` return.

Warning

Unpredictable results will ensue if the function that executed `setjmp` has itself returned or if *env* was never set by a call to `setjmp`.

Related functions

`setjmp`

lrand48

```
long lrand48 (void);
```

`Lrand48` returns a pseudo-random number uniformly distributed over the range 0 to 2,147,483,647.

The random-number generator should be seeded using one of the seed functions: `srand48`, `seed48`, or `lcong48`.

Warning

If the random-number generator is always seeded with the same value, or if no seed is introduced, the same series of pseudo-random numbers will be generated for every program execution.

Related functions

`drand48, erand48, jrand48, lcong48, mrand48, nrand48, rand, seed48, srand48`

lsearch

```
void *lsearch (const void *key, const
   void *table, unsigned nel,
   unsigned width, int (*compar)());
```

Headers

`search.h`

`Lsearch` searches an unordered array and inserts a new entry if it is not found. *Key* points to the entry to be found in the table, *table* points to the first element in the table, *nel* is the number of table entries, *width* is the length of an entry in bytes, and *compar* points to a user function declared as

```
int compar (const void *entry1, const
   void *entry2);
```

When *entry1* is equal to, greater than, or less than *entry2*, *compar* must return a zero, positive, or negative integer value, respectively.

Returns

a pointer to the table entry matching *key*. If no matching entry was found, entry is added to the end of the table, and a pointer to the new entry is returned.

Related functions

`lfind`

lseek

errno S

```
long lseek (int handle, long offset,
    int whence);
```

The file pointer of the file corresponding to *handle* is set to a new offset.

The offset is the sum of the values of *offset* and a value implied by *whence*, as follows:

`0`	Start of file
`1`	Current file position
`2`	End of file

The next read or write of the file will begin at the new position. If the file pointer is set beyond the end of file, the next read will return end of file, whereas a write will increase the file length accordingly. The use of `lseek` and `write` may introduce holes into the file by skipping some areas while writing into others.

Returns

the new value of the file pointer; –1 on error.

Warning

Some files cannot be repositioned. In these cases, the current file pointer is undefined, the value returned by `lseek` is meaningless, and the `lseek` has no effect.

Related functions

`creat, fseek, open`

mallinfo

-lmalloc

```
struct mallinfo mallinfo (void);
```

Headers

`malloc.h`

Returns

a `mallinfo` struct

The `mallinfo` structure contains the following members:

`arena`	Total number of bytes available for allocation
`ordblks`	Number of ordinary blocks allocated
`smblks`	Number of small blocks allocated
`hblkhd`	Number of bytes in holding-block headers
`hblks`	Number of holding blocks
`usmblks`	Number of bytes allocated in small blocks
`fsmblks`	Number of bytes in free small blocks
`uordblks`	Number of bytes allocated in ordinary blocks
`fordblks`	Number of bytes in free ordinary blocks
`keepcost`	Space penalty if M_KEEP option is in force

Related functions

`malloc, mallopt`

malloc

errno lmalloc

```
void *malloc (size_t size);
```

Headers

`malloc.h`

Returns

a pointer to an area of storage at least *size* bytes in length, properly aligned for any data type. NULL is returned if *size* cannot be allocated.

Two versions of `malloc` are available— one from the standard library and one from the *malloc* library. The latter is obtained when `-lmalloc` is supplied on the `cc` command. The standard version optimizes memory use, whereas `-lmalloc` optimizes execution speed.

Warning

Accesses to storage outside the range of allocated addresses may cause abnormal termination. The area returned by `malloc` contains unpredictable values.

Related functions

`calloc, free, mallopt, memset, realloc`

mallopt

-lmalloc

```
int mallopt (int cmd, int value);
```

Headers

`malloc.h`

`Mallopt` is used to modify the algorithm used by `malloc`. It may not be called after the first small block has been allocated.

For *cmd*, specify one of the following values defined in `malloc.h`:

M_MXFAST	sets *maxfast* to *value*.
M_NLBLKS	sets *numlbks* to *value*.
M_GRAIN	sets *grain* to *value*. *Value* will be rounded to assure proper alignment.
M_KEEP	causes data in a storage block released by *free* to be retained until reallocated.

Returns

a non-zero value if either *cmd* or *value* is invalid, or if storage allocation has already occurred; otherwise, returns zero.

Related functions

`calloc, free, mallinfo, malloc, realloc`

memccpy

```
char *memccpy (void *s1, const void
    *s2, int c, int n);
```

Headers

`memory.h`

`Memccpy` copies characters from the array pointed to by *s2* to the array pointed to by *s1*. Copying stops when the character *c* has been copied, or *n* characters have been copied.

Returns

a pointer to the character following *c* in *s1*; NULL, if *c* was not found.

Warning

Neither *s1* nor *s2* may be the NULL pointer.

Related functions

`memchr, memcmp, memcpy, memset, strcpy, strncpy`

memchr

```
char *memchr (const char *s, int c,
    int n);
```

Headers

`memory.h`

Returns

a pointer to the first occurrence of *c* in the *n*-element character array pointed to by *s*; the NULL pointer, if *c* is not found.

Warning

Result is undefined if *s* is the NULL pointer.

Related functions

memccpy, memcmp, memcpy, memset, strchr

memcmp

```
int memcmp (const void *s1, const void
    *s2, int n);
```

Headers

memory.h

Returns

When *s1* is equal to, greater than, or less than *s2*, *compar* must return a zero, positive, or negative integer value, respectively.

Exactly *n* characters are compared and any null characters found are treated as data characters.

Warning

Result is not defined if either *s1* or *s2* is NULL.

Related functions

memccpy, memchr, memcpy, memset, strcmp, strncmp

memcpy

```
char *memcpy (void *s1, const void
    *s2, int n);
```

Headers

memory.h

Memcpy copies *n* characters from the array pointed to by *s2* to the array pointed to by *s1*.

Returns

s1

Warning

Result is not defined if either *s1* or *s2* is NULL.

Related functions

`memccpy, memchr, memcmp, memset, strcpy, strncpy`

memset

```
char *memset (void *s, int c, int n);
```

Headers

`memory.h`

`Memset` copies *n* occurrences of character *c* to the array pointed to by *s*.

Returns

s

Warning

Result is not defined if *s* is NULL.

Related functions

`memccpy, memchr, memcmp, memcpy`

mkdir

errno S R3

```
int mkdir (const char *path, int
    mode);
```

A new directory is created with a pathname of *path*. Permissions of the directory are set to the 12 low-order bits of *mode* as modified by the process file-creation mask (see `umask`). Owner-ID and group-ID of new directory are set to effective user-ID and effective group-ID of calling process, respectively. The request will fail if the pathname already exists or if the caller does not have write permission in the parent directory.

Returns

0 if successful; –1 otherwise.

Warning

The `mkdir` system call is not a direct substitute for command invocation of `/bin/mkdir`, since the latter command creates the new directory, the real-user-ID, and the real-group-ID of calling process, respectively.

Related functions

`chmod, creat, mknod, rmdir, umask`

mktemp

```
char *mktemp (char *template);
```

Use `mktemp` to generate a unique filename for temporary files. The last six characters of the string pointed to by *template* should be `XXXXXX`. The six X's will be replaced by an arbitrarily chosen letter and the 5-digit current process-ID.

Returns

value of *template*.

Warning

The arbitrary letter is chosen from a list internal to `mktemp` to ensure that no two file names will be the same. If many file names are generated, `mktemp` can run out of letters. This naming procedure cannot guarantee that generated file names are unique; only that file names generated by `mktemp` will be unique.

Related functions

`tmpfile, tmpnam`

modf

```
double modf (double dn, double *iptr);
```

Returns

the fractional part of *dn*. The integer part is stored at the location pointed to by *iptr*.

mrand48

```
long mrand48 (void);
```

`Mrand48` returns a pseudo-random number distributed over the range –2,147,483,648 to 2,147,483,647. The generator should be seeded using one of the seed functions `srand48`, `seed48`, or `lcong48`.

Warning

If the generator is always seeded with the same value, or if no seed is introduced, the same series of numbers will be generated for every execution.

Related functions

`drand48, erand48, jrand48, lcong48, lrand48, nrand48, rand, seed48, srand48`

nice

errno S KE

```
int nice (int incr);
```

`Nice` increases or decreases the scheduling priority of the calling process by *incr*, to a maximum value of 39 or a minimum value of 0. Smaller values of scheduling priority increase the CPU share of the calling process; larger values reduce the share consumed.

The effective user-ID must be super-user if *incr* is negative or greater than 40.

Returns

20 less than the new scheduling priority; –1 if unsuccessful.

nrand48

```
long nrand48 (unsigned short
    lvalue[3]);
```

`Nrand48` returns a pseudo-random number uniformly distributed over the range 0 to 2,147,483,647.

The array pointed to by *lvalue* must contain a 48-bit value prior to invocation; upon return, it contains the *X*-value that will be used to generate the next random number. Some value should be introduced into the array prior to calling `nrand48`.

Multiple independent random-number series can be generated using a separate *lvalue* array for each series.

Related functions

`drand48, erand48, jrand48, lcong48, lrand48, mrand48, rand, seed48, srand48`

open

errno S

```
int open (const char *path, int
    oflags, int mode);
```

Headers

`fcntl.h`

An unused file descriptor is chosen and initialized for subsequent reading and writing of the file named by *path*. The file pointer is set to the beginning of the file, and the close-on-exec flag is set to zero.

The actions taken by `open` are determined by the bits of *oflags*, defined in fcntl.h as follows:

O_RDONLY	Open for read access.
O_WRONLY	Open for write access.
O_RDWR	Opened for both read and write.
O_APPEND	Causes the file pointer to be reset to end of file for each write request.
O_CREAT	Causes the file to be created if it does not already exist. The *mode* argument must specify the 12 low-order bits of file-access permissions (see `chmod`).
O_EXCL	Causes open to fail if the file already exists and O_CREAT is also specified.
O_NDELAY	Causes immediate return when input is not available (see `read` and `write`).
O_SYNC	Delays return from `write` request until data is actually written.
O_TRUNC	If the file exists, its length is set to 0.

Only one of the O_RDONLY, O_WRONLY, and O_RDWR values may be specified in *oflags*. Flag values may be combined by OR'ing the desired flags.

Returns

the file handle, if successful; –1 otherwise.

Warning

The system imposes a limit (usually 20) on the number of files that may be open simultaneously by any one process. Program design should minimize the number of files used. The standard input, standard output, and standard error files count toward this limit.

Related functions

`close, chmod, creat, lseek, read, umask, write`

opendir

errno R3

```
DIR *opendir (const char *path);
```

Headers

`sys/types.h, dirent.h`

The directory named by *path* is opened for reading, and the current location is set to the first entry. The file named by *path* must be a directory.

Once opened, active directory entries can be read using `readdir`; the current location can be controlled with `seekdir`, `telldir`, and `rewinddir`. The directory must be closed with `closedir`.

Returns

a pointer to a DIR structure allocated using `malloc`; NULL if open is unsuccessful.

Related functions

`closedir, readdir, rewinddir, seekdir, telldir`

pause

errno S

```
int pause (void);
```

`Pause` suspends execution of the calling process until a signal is received, but the result of the signal is determined by the action set for that signal (see `signal`).

Related functions

`alarm, kill, signal, wait`

pclose

```
int pclose (FILE *stream);
```

Headers

`stdio.h`

The stream file pointed to by *stream* (which must be one side of a pipe opened by `popen`) is closed after waiting for termination of the associated process.

Returns

the exit status of the command invoked by `popen`.

Related functions

`fclose, popen, wait`

perror

```
void perror (const char *msg);
```

`Perror` writes an error message corresponding to the current value of *errno* to the standard-error file. The message is preceded by the string pointed to by *msg*.

Related functions

`errno, sys_errlist, sys_nerr`

pipe

errno S

```
int pipe (int handle[2]);
```

An I/O channel called a *pipe* is created; a pipe consists of two file descriptors, one opened for reading and one opened for writing. The handle of the read file descriptor is stored in *handle[0]*; the handle of the write file descriptor is stored in *handle[1]*.

Data written to pipe is accumulated in an internal system buffer up to 5,120 bytes long; when the buffer is full, the next `write` to pipe will suspend the calling process.

Read requests are satisfied up to the amount of data in the buffer. If the buffer is empty, the caller is suspended until data is written to the pipe. Either handle may be closed first. However, if the read file descriptor is closed and data is then written to the pipe, the SIGPIPE signal is posted to the writing process. This condition (called a *broken pipe*) indicates that no process is available to read the data being written to the pipe.

Returns

0 if successful; –1 otherwise.

Warning

Lseek cannot be used to set the file pointer of a pipe forward or back; data must be read in the same sequence it is written.

Related functions

`close, read, write`

popen

errno

```
FILE *popen (const char *command,
   const char *type);
```

Headers

`stdio.h`

`Popen` passes the string *command* to `/bin/sh` for execution. If *type* points to the string "r," the standard output of the command is opened for reading; reading the FILE pointer returned by `popen` will read the output of the command. If *type* points to the string "w," the standard input of the command is opened for writing, and writes to the FILE pointer returned by `popen` will pass input to the command.

Returns

a pointer to an opened FILE block; NULL if either `fork` or `exec` failed.

The FILE pointer returned by `popen` must be closed using `pclose`, which will wait for the command to complete and return its exit status.

Warning

The exit status of the invoked command is not known until `pclose` is called. Errors found by the command cannot be recognized until the command's exit status is retrieved from `pclose`.

Related functions

`fopen, pclose, pipe`

pow

errno -lm

```
double pow (double x, double y);
```

Headers

`math.h`

Returns

x raised to the power of *y*.

Warning

If the result would over- or underflow, returns +-HUGE or 0, respectively, and sets *errno* to ERANGE. Sets *errno* to EDOM if *x* is 0 and *y* is negative or if *x* is negative and *y* is not an integer.

printf

errno

```
int printf (const char *format, ...);
```

Headers

`stdio.h`

Values taken from the argument list are formatted according to specifications contained in the string *format*, and the result is written to standard output. The format string consists of *message characters* and *format specifiers*. Message characters are output without further processing.

A *format specifier* is a substring of the general form

```
%[flags][width][.prec]type
```

As each format specifier is encountered, successive arguments of `printf` are fetched and converted. Excess arguments are ignored.

Flag is –, +, *0*, #, or *blank*. – causes a result to be left-justified in a field of *width* characters; + and *blank* both force the result to contain a sign; *0* causes a numeric result to be padded on the left with zeros; # causes a special effect (described in the following list of *type* characters and their meanings).

Width is an optional string of digits or an * denoting the size of the output field. The result will be left- or right-justified in the field unless the –flag is present or width is too short. An * causes width to be taken from argument list; corresponding argument must be of type `int`.

Prec is a string of digits denoting how many fractional digits appear in a floating-point result, or number of digits in an integer. *Prec* may be specified as *.

Type characters and their meanings follow:

- *%* Prints one % for each %% in format string
- *c* Prints ASCII character matching integer argument
- *d* Integer argument is converted to decimal digits, prefixed with a minus sign if argument is negative.
- *e,E* Floating-point argument is converted to exponential notation (+9.999e+99). # flag forces an integral result to contain a decimal point.
- *f* Floating-point argument is converted to a fixed-point number (–ddd.ddd) with *prec* fractional digits. If *prec* is specified as 0, both decimal point and fractional digits are dropped from result. # flag forces result to contain a decimal point.

g,G Floating-point argument is converted to either *f* or *e* (*E*) format, depending on value of argument. # flag forces result to contain a decimal point, and trailing zeros to be retained.

o Integer argument is converted to an unsigned octal digit string. # flag adds zero prefix.

s Corresponding argument is interpreted as pointer to character string. The *prec* value, if present, specifies a maximum number of characters to be printed. String is right-aligned in field of *width* characters.

u Integer argument is interpreted as an unsigned number and converted to a decimal digit string.

x,X Integer argument is converted to an unsigned hexadecimal digit string, extended with 0's or truncated on left to a length of *prec*, and prefixed with 0x or 0X if # flag is present.

For conversion types *duoxX*, an *h* or *l* may precede conversion character, with *h* signifying a half-size argument (`short int`) and *l* signifying `long int`. For conversion types *eEfgG*, an *h* prefix signifies an argument of type `float`, whereas an *l* signifies a `double` argument. Default is `double`.

Returns

number of characters written to standard output; –1 on error

Warning

If the number of arguments following *format* is less than the number of format specifiers, `printf` will fetch garbage argument values from the stack. The user must ensure agreement between the description of arguments and the actual type of arguments supplied.

Related functions

`ecvt, fprintf, putc, puts, scanf, sprintf, vprintf`

putc

```
int putc (int c, FILE *stream);
```

Headers

`stdio.h`

`Putc` writes the character *c* to the stream file *stream*. The file pointer is advanced by one byte. The character is written immediately, unless the buffering mode for *stream* is *line* or *full* (see `setvbuf`).

Returns

value *c*; EOF on error

Warning

Putc is implemented as a macro.

Related functions

`fclose, ferror, fopen, fputc, fseek, getc, putchar, puts, setbuf`

putchar

errno

```
int putchar (int c);
```

Headers

`stdio.h`

`Putchar` differs from `putc` only in that output is written to the standard output stream by default.

Returns

value *c*

Related functions

`getchar, putc`

putenv

```
int putenv (const char *string);
```

The string pointed to by *string* is added to the program environment. *String* is assumed to be in the format `name=value` where *name* is a variable name and *value* is value of the variable. No space should occur between *name* and the = delimiter.

If *name* already occurs in the program, the existing string is dropped and replaced with the new string.

Returns

zero if successful. A non-zero value indicates that space to expand the environment pointer table could not be acquired; in this case, the string has not been added.

Warning

1. Modifying the character array pointed to by *string* will alter the environment.
2. Certain naming restrictions may apply if the environment variable is referenced by shell programs.

Related functions

`environ, execle, getenv`

puts

errno

```
int puts (const char *string);
```

Headers

`stdio.h`

The string pointed to by *string* is written to the standard output file, followed by a newline character. The ending null character is not written.

Returns

EOF on error; otherwise, zero

Warning

`Puts` writes a trailing newline character, whereas `fputs` does not.

Related functions

`ferror, fopen, fputs, gets, putchar`

putw

```
int putw (int w, FILE *stream);
```

Headers

`stdio.h`

`Putw` writes the bytes of the integer *w* to *stream*. The file pointer is advanced by the size of an integer. No alignment of the file pointer occurs.

Returns

zero if successful; otherwise, a non-zero value

Warning

The ordering of bytes written to the output file is determined by the machine and compiler implementation; use `printf` when portability is desired.

Related functions

`fclose, ferror, fopen, fseek, fwrite, getw, printf, putc, setbuf`

qsort

```
void qsort (const void *table,
    unsigned nel, unsigned width, int
    (*compar)());
```

`Qsort` sorts elements of array pointed to by *table* by using QuickSort algorithm. The resulting order of elements in array is determined by the user comparison function *compar*.

Nel is number of entries in table, *width* is length of an element of array in bytes, and *compar* is a user function with an assumed declaration of

```
int compar (const void *entry1,
  const void *entry2);
```

When *entry1* is equal to, greater than, or less than *entry2*, *compar* must return a zero, positive, or negative integer value, respectively.

Related functions

`bsearch, lsearch, strcmp`

rand

```
int rand (void);
```

Returns

a random number in the range 0 to 32,767. The generated series is completely determined by the seed value previously introduced by `srand`.

Warning

The generator used by `rand` is not particularly good. Use one of the 48-bit generators instead.

Related functions

`drand48, srand`

read

errno S

```
int read (int handle, void *buffer,
    unsigned len);
```

Data is read from the file associated with *handle* and stored in consecutive positions of *buffer* until *len* bytes have been stored, end of file is reached, or (for terminals) all available buffered data has been read.

For block-special devices and files stored on such devices, reading begins at the byte offset given by the file pointer. Character-special files cannot be positioned and the file pointer is undefined; such files are read beginning with the next position defined by the device.

If O_NDELAY is set, a read is terminated immediately and a value of 0 is returned if no data is available; otherwise, the calling process is suspended until data is available or, for a pipe, the pipe is closed.

Returns

0 if no data was stored (usually signifies end of file); –1 if an error occurred; or number of bytes stored in *buffer*.

Warning

When `read` is interrupted, the return value will be –1 and *errno* will specify EINTR. `Read` should be retried until a completion other than EINTR is returned.

Related functions

`creat, fcntl, ioctl, open, pipe`

readdir

errno R3

```
struct dirent *readdir (DIR *dirp);
```

Headers

`sys/types.h, dirent.h`

The directory entry at the current location is read from the directory file pointed to by *dirp*, the value of which must have been obtained from a previous call to `opendir`. The current directory location is advanced to the entry following that returned by `readdir`. If the directory entry is not active, successive entries are skipped until an active entry or end of directory is found. `Readdir` does not return inactive directory entries.

Returns

a pointer to a `struct dirent` containing the directory entry; a NULL pointer if end of directory was found or if the current directory location is invalid because of a previous `seekdir` (see `dirent.h`).

Related functions

`closedir, opendir, rewinddir, seekdir, telldir, dirent.h`

realloc

errno

```
void *realloc (void *area, size_t
   size);
```

Headers

`malloc.h`

The storage area pointed to by *area* is extended (or reduced) to a length of *size* bytes. If the area cannot be extended, the original area is released by a call to `free`, a new storage block of the requested size is allocated, and the contents of the original area are copied to the new area.

Returns

a pointer to an area of storage at least *size* bytes in length, properly aligned for any data type. NULL is returned if the space cannot be allocated.

Warning

1. If the requested storage could not be allocated, the previous area has already been released and can no longer be accessed.

2. Accesses outside the range of the allocated addresses may cause abnormal termination.
3. Undefined results will occur if the value of *area* is not a pointer value previously returned by `malloc`, `calloc`, or `realloc`.

Related functions

`calloc, free, malloc`

rewind

```
void rewind (FILE *stream);
```

Headers

`stdio.h`

`Rewind` resets the current position of the *stream* file to the beginning of the file. Any EOF indication is cleared.

Related functions

`fseek, ftell`

rewindir

R3

```
void rewinddir (DIR *dirp);
```

Headers

`sys/types.h, dirent.h`

The current location of the directory file associated with *dirp* is set to the first entry of the directory.

Warning

`Rewinddir` is implemented as a macro.

Related functions

`closedir, opendir, readdir, seekdir, telldir, dirent.h`

rmdir

errno S R3

```
int rmdir (const char *path);
```

The directory named by *path* is removed if it is empty, not a mount point, not the current directory of a process, and the calling process' parent directory has write permission.

Returns

0 if successful; –1 otherwise

Related functions

`mkdir, unlink`

scanf

errno

```
int scanf (const char *format, ...);
```

Headers

`stdio.h`

`Scanf` reads string data from the standard input file and converts the strings found into the equivalent internal representation. Reading continues until an input character fails to match the corresponding format specification, end of format string is reached, or EOF is found.

The character string pointed to by *format* controls data conversion as follows:

Characters other than % must be matched by characters from the input stream. A whitespace character in the format string causes any number of whitespace characters in the input stream to be skipped. A % in the format string begins a format specifier, which causes data conversion to occur and a converted result to be stored at a user-defined location. Each format specifier causes the next argument of `scanf` to be fetched and used as a pointer to store the conversion result. The pointer's type is implied by the format specifier. The number of arguments following the format must be at least as large as the number of format specifiers in the format string, with the following exception:

The syntax of the format specifier is

```
%[*][width]type
```

If the optional * character is present, data conversion occurs normally but the result is not stored, and the pointer argument to `scanf` must be omitted. A specifier of this kind causes input data to be skipped, while confirming that it matches an expected format.

If optional *width* value is present, at most that number of characters will be taken from the input string and converted. *Width* value can be used to limit the amount of data stored (for types *c*, *s*, and *[*), or to break apart fields that are adjacent in input stream. Excess input characters that otherwise would have been processed by the format specifier are left on the input stream to be processed by the next format specifier.

Type specifies the kind of conversion to be performed. It is made up of an optional size modifier and a type character. *l* denotes a long or double result value, and *h* denotes a short or float result value. The result's default size is in the following list.

A *type* character can be one of the following:

% Current input character is matched against %. No pointer argument should be provided.

d,u String of digits is expected, optionally beginning with minus sign. Sign and digits are converted to a value; result is in signed or unsigned integer.

o String of octal digits is expected. Digits are converted and result is in signed or unsigned integer.

x String of hexadecimal digits is expected. Letters [a-f] and [A-F] are taken to mean digit values 10-15. Digits are converted and result is stored in signed or unsigned integer.

e,f,g Input string is expected to be an external floating-point number. String may be prefixed with a sign character, and may be suffixed with an *e* or *E*, optionally followed by a sign character, followed by one or more digits. Number itself may contain one decimal point. String is converted and stored in `float` item pointed to by next `scanf` argument.

s Character string is expected. String is ended by first whitespace character following start of string. Corresponding argument must point to a character array large enough to contain string and an ending null (\0) character.

c Next input character (or *width* input characters) is stored in character array pointed to by corresponding `scanf` argument. Whitespace characters are stored if encountered. No null character is appended.

[Opening bracket begins character-set specification; must end with matching *]*. Characters between brackets specify a character set. Input is read and stored up to first character not appearing in set, and trailing null character is appended. Range of characters can be indicated by expression *x-y*. If bracketed expression begins with ^, character set is all ASCII characters not in bracketed expression. To include a *]* in character set, place it immediately after opening *[* or *[^*. No skipping of space occurs before or after processing. Corresponding argument of `scanf` must be pointer to character array.

Returns

number of result values converted and stored, or EOF if end of input stream was reached before any values were stored. Note that successful matching of pattern characters in format string does not affect count returned.

Related functions

getc, printf, strtod, strtol

seed48

```
unsigned short *seed48 (unsigned short
    seed[3]);
```

The 48-bit value contained in the array *seed* is set into the *X*-value used internally by drand48, lrand48, and mrand48. A given 48-bit value will always cause the same series of numbers to be generated.

Returns

a pointer to the three-element array internal to seed48 containing the 48-bit *X*-value last used for generating a random number. This value could be saved and later used as a seed value to restart an interrupted program.

Related functions

drand48, erand48, jrand48, lcong48, lrand48, mrand48, nrand48, rand, srand48

seekdir

R3

```
void seekdir (DIR *dirp, long loc);
```

Headers

sys/types.h, dirent.h

The current location of the directory file associated with *dirp* is set to *loc*. The value of *loc* should have been obtained previously from `telldir`. Validity is not tested until `readdir` attempt to use the location.

Related functions

`closedir, opendir, readdir, rewinddir, telldir, dirent.h`

setbuf

```
int setbuf (FILE *stream, char *buf);
```

Headers

`stdio.h`

The character array pointed to by *buf* is substituted for the automatically acquired buffer associated with stream file *stream*. The size of the new buffer must be equal to the value of BUFSIZ defined in `stdio.h`. If *buf* is NULL, the stream will be unbuffered.

Returns

zero if successful; otherwise, non-zero

Warning

Setbuf must be called before the first read or write to *stream*.

Related functions

`fopen, setvbuf`

setgid

errno S

```
int setgid (int gid);
```

If invoked by super-user, `setgid` sets both real and effective group-ID of calling process to value of *gid*.

If invoked by the general user, `setgid` sets the effective group-ID of the calling process to the value of *gid*. The real group-ID remains unchanged. The request will fail unless *gid* is either the real group-ID of the calling process or the saved set-group-ID found by `exec`.

Returns

0 if successful; –1 otherwise

Related functions

`chmod, exec, getegid, getgid, setuid`

setjmp

```
int setjmp (jmp_buf env);
```

Headers

`setjmp.h`

Applications typically consist of many functions that call each other to perform the application task, but error handling can be awkward when an error is detected in a deeply nested call. `Setjmp` can be used to transfer control to a function other than the calling function.

The stack of the function calling `setjmp` is saved in the variable *env* of type `jmp_buf`. (Type name `jmp_buf` is defined in `setjmp.h`.) As long as the function that called `setjmp` does not return, `longjmp` can be used to restore the stack saved by `setjmp`. A lower-level function using `longjmp` therefore appears to return from `setjmp` and does not return to the function that called it.

Returns

zero, but when `longjmp` is used, the return value will appear to be non-zero; the actual return value is obtained from `longjmp`. Normally, applications will establish a convention for the significance of non-zero return values set via `longjmp`.

Warning

The function executing `setjmp` must remain active; `setjmp` should therefore be issued in one of the program's high-level functions.

Related functions

`longjmp`

setpgrp

S

```
int setpgrp (void);
```

The process group-ID is set to the same value as the process-ID of the calling process.

Returns

new process group-ID

Related functions

`getpgrp, signal`

setpwent

```
void setpwent (void);
   void setspent (void);
```

The internal file used by `getpwent` is repositioned to its beginning; the next call to `getpwent` will return the first line of `/etc/passwd`. Use `setpwent` when repeated searches of the password file are required.

`Setspent` performs the equivalent function for the `/etc/shadow` file (*R3 only*).

Related functions

`endpwent, getpwent`

setuid

errno S

```
int setuid (int uid);
```

If invoked by the super-user, `setuid` sets both the real and effective user-ID of the calling process to *uid*.

If invoked by the general user, `setuid` sets the effective user-ID of the calling process to the value of *uid*. The real user-ID remains unchanged. The request will fail unless *uid* is either the real user-ID of the calling process, or the saved set-user-ID found by `exec`.

Returns

0 if successful; –1 otherwise

Related functions

`chmod, exec, geteuid, getuid, setgid, setpgrp`

setvbuf

```
int setvbuf (FILE *stream, char *buf,
   int type, int size);
```

Headers

`stdio.h`

`Setvbuf` replaces the automatic buffer of *stream* with user-provided buffer *buf*. *Size* specifies size in bytes of new buffer.

Type specifies type of buffering to be used for *stream*, and must be one of the following values defined in `stdio.h`:

_IOFBF Full buffering. If reading, buffer will be filled only when it is empty; if writing, buffer is flushed only when it is full.

_IOLBF Line buffering. Buffer is filled or flushed when complete line has been processed.

_IONBF No buffering. Reading and writing occur immediately. Values of *buf* and *size* are ignored.

Optimum size for a stream buffer is defined in `stdio.h`.

Returns

non-zero value on error; otherwise, zero

Related functions

`fopen, setbuf`

signal

errno S

```
void (*signal (int sig, void
    (*func)())) ()
```

Headers

`signal.h`

`Signal` defines the action to occur (*func*) when signal *sig* is posted to the calling process. Valid signal names (defined in `signal.h`) are the following:

Name	Nmbr	Meaning
SIGHUP	1	Hangup
SIGINT	2	Interrupt
SIGQUIT	3	Quit
SIGILL	4*	Illegal instruction (not reset)
SIGTRAP	5*	Trace interrupt (not reset)
SIGIOT	6*	IOT instruction
SIGEMT	7*	EMT instruction
SIGFPE	8*	Floating-point exception
SIGKILL	9	Kill (cannot be reset or ignored)
SIGBUS	10*	Bus error
SIGSEGV	11*	Segmentation violation

Name	*Nmbr*	*Meaning*
SISSYS	12*	Invalid argument to system call
SIGPIPE	13	Broken pipe
SIGALRM	14	Process alarm clock
SIGTERM	15	Software termination
SIGUSR1	16	User defined
SIGUSR2	17	User defined
SIGCLD	18	Death of a child process
SIGPWR	19	Power failure

The value of *func* may be one of the following:

SIG_DFL Process is terminated as if `exit` were called. Signals marked with an asterisk cause a *core* file to be written to the current directory.

SIG_IGN Signal is ignored. (SIGKILL cannot be ignored.)

func Function pointed to by *func* is invoked as if it were called at the point of interruption, after resetting the signal action to SIG_DFL. The declaration of *func* is

```
void func (int sig)
```

If *func* returns, the process resumes execution from the point of interruption. The original signal action is not restored.

The default action for all signals is SIG_DFL.

Returns

the previous action value for *sig*, if successful; –1 otherwise

Warning

If a signal is raised during one of the system calls `open` or `ioctl` (except for disk accesses), `read`, `write`, `pause`, or `wait`, the system call may return –1 and set *errno* to EINTR. The interrupted system call may be repeated without loss of data or improper processing.

Related functions

`execl, fork, kill, pause, wait`

sin

errno -lm

```
double sin (double x);
```

Headers

`math.h`

Returns

trigonometric sine of argument *x* in radians

sinh

errno -lm

```
double sinh (double x);
```

Headers

`math.h`

Returns

hyperbolic sine of *x*

sleep

```
unsigned sleep (unsigned seconds);
```

Use `sleep` to suspend program execution for a real-time interval of *sleep* seconds. The time slept may be longer if other system activity delays interruptions. Although `sleep` uses the process alarm clock, any value that may have been set is saved and restored by `sleep`.

Returns

the number of seconds remaining to be slept which could not be slept because of the interruption signal.

Warning

A signal-catching routine set up for SIGALRM will be entered as a result of `sleep` execution.

Related functions

`alarm, pause, signal`

sprintf

errno

```
int sprintf (char *buf, const char
    *format, ...);
```

Headers

`stdio.h`

`Sprintf` differs from `printf` in that the result string is stored in *buf*, instead of being written to an output file. The null character ('\0') is placed at the end of the result string.

Returns

number of characters stored in *buf*, exclusive of trailing null character

Warning

`Sprintf` will overrun the end of the array pointed to by *buf* if it is too short to contain the result string.

Related functions

`ecvt, fprintf, printf`

sqrt

errno -lm

```
double sqrt (double x);
```

Headers

math.h

Returns

square-root of *x*

Warning

Returns 0 and sets *errno* to EDOM if *x* is negative.

srand

```
void srand (unsigned int seed);
```

`Srand` seeds `rand`. If `srand` is not called, `rand` uses the default initial seed of 1.

Related functions

rand

srand48

```
void srand48 (long seed);
```

The 32 high-order bits of the *X*-value used internally by `drand48`, `lrand48`, and `mrand48` is initialized to *seed*. The 16 low-order bits are set to an arbitrary value.

Related functions

drand48, erand48, jrand48, lcong48, lrand48, mrand48, nrand48, rand, seed48

sscanf

errno

```
int sscanf (const char *string, const
   char *format, ...);
```

Headers

`stdio.h`

`Sscanf` is identical to `scanf` except that `sscanf` scans the string pointed to by *string* instead of standard input. *String* is not altered.

Returns

the number of values converted and stored, which can be zero if an early mismatch occurred.

Related functions

`fclose, ferror, fopen, fread, getc, scanf, sscanf`

stat

errno S

```
int stat (const char *path, struct
   stat *buf);
```

Headers

`sys/types.h, sys/stat.h`

`Stat` returns information about the file *path* in *buf*. The format of the `stat` struct is defined in `stat.h`. The calling process must have search permission for all directories in *path*; read permission is not required.

Returns

0 if successful; –1 otherwise

Related functions

`access, fstat, stat.h`

strcat

```
char *strcat (const char *s1, const
   char *s2);
```

Headers

string.h

The string *s2* is copied to the end of *s1*, forming the concatenation of the two original strings. The array *s1* must be large enough to contain both strings plus a trailing null character.

Returns

pointer *s1*

Warning

The result is not defined if either argument is NULL.

Related functions

strchr, strcmp, strcpy, strcspn, strlen, strncat, strncmp, strncpy, strpbrk, strrchr, strspn, strtok

strchr

```
char *strchr (const char *s, int c);
```

Headers

string.h

Returns

pointer to the first occurrence of character *c* in string *s*, or a NULL pointer if character *c* does not occur in *s*. The null character ('\0') will always be found.

Warning

Result is undefined if *s* is NULL.

Related functions

`strcat, strcmp, strcpy, strcspn, strlen, strncat, strncmp, strncpy, strpbrk, strrchr, strspn, strtok`

strcmp

```
int strcmp (const char *s1, const char
   *s2);
```

Headers

`string.h`

String *s1* is compared to string *s2*.

Returns

When *s1* is equal to, greater than, or less than *s2*, *compar* must return a zero, positive, or negative integer value, respectively.

Warning

Result is undefined if either argument is NULL.

Related functions

`strcat, strchr, strcpy, strcspn, strlen, strncat, strncmp, strncpy, strpbrk, strrchr, strspn, strtok`

strcpy

```
char *strcpy (const char *s1, const
   char *s2);
```

Headers

`string.h`

The string *s2* is copied to *s1*. The user is responsible for ensuring that the character array *s1* is large enough to contain the string to be copied plus a trailing null.

Returns

pointer *s1*

Warning

Result is undefined if either argument is NULL.

Related functions

```
strcat, strchr, strcmp, strcspn,
strlen, strncat, strncmp, strncpy,
strpbrk, strrchr, strspn, strtok
```

strcspn

```
int strcspn (const char *s1, const
   char *s2);
```

Headers

```
string.h
```

Returns

length of the initial substring of *s1* that consists only of the characters not in *s2*.

Warning

Result is undefined if either argument is NULL.

Related functions

```
strcat, strchr, strcmp, strcpy,
strlen, strncat, strncmp, strncpy,
strpbrk, strrchr, strspn, strtok
```

strdup

R3

```
char *strdup (const char *s);
```

Headers

`string.h`

Returns

pointer to a copy of string *s* made in storage allocated by `malloc`; when no longer required, the copy should be released (use `free`). Returns NULL if allocation fails.

Warning

Result is undefined if *s* is NULL.

Related functions

`free, malloc strcpy, strncpy`

strlen

```
int strlen (const char *s);
```

Headers

`string.h`

Returns

length of string *s*, excluding the trailing null character

Warning

Result is undefined if *s* is NULL.

Related functions

```
strcat, strchr, strcmp, strcpy,
strcspn, strncat, strncmp, strncpy,
strpbrk, strrchr, strspn, strtok
```

strncat

```
char *strncat (const char *s1, const
    char *s2, int n);
```

Headers

string.h

String *s2* (up to *n* characters) is copied to the end of string *s1*. The character array *s1* must be large enough to contain the concatenated string plus a trailing null.

Returns

pointer *s1*

Warning

Result is undefined if either argument is NULL.

Related functions

strcat, strchr, strcmp, strcpy, strcspn, strlen, strncmp, strncpy, strpbrk, strrchr, strspn, strtok

strncmp

```
int strncmp (const char *s1, const
    char *s2, int n);
```

Headers

string.h

Returns

When *s1* is equal to, greater than, or less than *s2*, *compar* must return a zero, positive, or negative integer value, respectively.

Warning

Result is undefined if either argument is NULL.

Related functions

`strcat, strchr, strcpy, strcspn, strlen, strncat, strncmp, strncpy, strpbrk, strrchr, strspn, strtok`

strncpy

```
char *strncpy (const char *s1, const
   char *s2, int n);
```

Headers

`string.h`

The string *s2* is copied to the array *s1*.

The result is truncated or padded with nulls to a length of *n* characters. No trailing null is stored unless the string *s2* is less than *n* characters long.

Returns

pointer *s1*

Warning

Result is undefined if either argument is NULL.

Related functions

`strcat, strchr, strcmp, strcpy, strcspn, strlen, strncat, strncmp, strpbrk, strrchr, strspn, strtok`

strpbrk

```
char *strpbrk (const char *s1, const
   char s2);
```

Headers

`string.h`

Returns

pointer to the first occurrence of a character in *s1* that matches any character in *s2*; NULL if none of the characters in *s2* occur in *s1*.

Warning

Result is undefined if either argument is NULL.

Related functions

strcat, strchr, strcmp, strcpy, strcspn, strlen, strncat, strncmp, strncpy, strrchr, strspn, strtok

strrchr

```
char *strrchr (const char *s, int c);
```

Headers

string.h

Returns

pointer to the last occurrence of character *c* in string *s*; NULL if *c* does not occur in *s*.

Warning

Result is undefined if *s* is NULL.

Related functions

strcat, strchr, strcmp, strcpy, strcspn, strlen, strncat, strncmp, strncpy, strpbrk, strspn, strtok

strspn

```
int strspn (const char *s1, const char
    *s2);
```

Headers

```
string.h
```

Returns

length of the initial substring of *s1* that consists only of characters from *s2*.

Warning

Result is undefined if either argument is NULL.

Related functions

```
strcat, strchr, strcmp, strcpy,
strcspn, strlen, strncat, strncmp,
strncpy, strpbrk, strrchr, strtok
```

strtod

errno

```
double strtod (const char *string,
   char **ptr);
```

Returns

the double-precision number represented by *string*. *String* may contain leading spaces, a sign character, one or more digits containing a decimal point, and an exponent. Conversion is stopped by the first illegal character in *string*; a pointer to this character is stored in the location pointed to by *ptr* (unless *ptr* is NULL).

Warning

If an over- or underflow would occur, HUGE or zero is returned and *errno* is set to EDOM.

Related functions

```
atof, scanf, strtol
```

strtok

```
char *strtok (char *text, const char
    *delims);
```

Headers

string.h

Strtok extracts the next token from *text*, where each token is separated by one or more delimiters in *delims*.

If *text* is the NULL pointer, search begins following the last token returned by strtok; otherwise, the search begins at *text*.

All initial occurrences of any character in *delims* are skipped. Strtok then returns the next string ending with any character in *delims*.

If the string pointed to by *text* contains none of the characters in *delims*, or *delims* is a string of length zero, the entire string is identified as a single token.

Returns

pointer to first character of the token; NULL if no more tokens can be found.

Related functions

strcat, strchr, strcmp, strcpy, strcspn, strlen, strncat, strncmp, strncpy, strpbrk, strrchr, strspn

strtol

```
long strtol (const char *string, char
    **ptr, int radix);
```

Returns

the long integer value of *string*. *String* may contain leading spaces, an optional sign, and one or more digits.

Conversion is stopped by the first illegal character in *string*; a pointer to this character is stored in the location pointed to by *ptr* (unless *ptr* is NULL).

Radix specifies the number base in which the number in *string* is expressed, and may be any value from 2-36 or zero. If *radix* is zero, the string determines its own radix: numbers beginning with a leading zero are assumed to be octal; those beginning with `0x` or `0X`, hexadecimal; those beginning with a non-zero digit, decimal.

Related functions

`atoi, atol, scanf, strtod`

sys_errlist

```
extern char *sys_errlist [];
```

Headers

`errno.h`

Sys_errlist is an array of pointers to null-terminated strings, such that when the array is indexed by a value of *errno*, a message text corresponding to the error is obtained.

`Perror` can be used to print the *sys_errlist* message corresponding to *errno* on *stderr*.

Related functions

`errno, sys_nerr, perror`

sys_nerr

```
extern int sys_nerr;
```

Headers

`errno.h`

The value of *sys_nerr* is the largest value of *errno* for which a message-text pointer can be found in *sys_errlist*.

Related functions

errno, sys_errlist, perror

system

errno

```
int system (const char *command);
```

The string *command* is passed to a new copy of the shell for execution as a command. The shell invoked is always /bin/sh to enhance the portability of programs; the -c option is used to limit shell execution solely to the command passed.

Returns

negative value if shell could not be invoked because fork or exec system calls failed; otherwise, return value is value returned by shell.

Related functions

execl, fork, popen

tan

errno -lm

```
double tan (double x);
```

Headers

math.h

Returns

trigonometric tangent of argument *x* in radians

tanh

errno -lm

```
double tanh (double x);
```

Headers

`math.h`

Returns

hyperbolic tangent of *x* .

tdelete

```
void *tdelete (void *key, void **root,
   int (*compar)());
```

Headers

`search.h`

`Tdelete` removes the item in the binary tree pointed to by **root* which matches *key*. The user function *compar* describes the ordering relation between items. (See `tsearch`.)

The matching item is removed by altering pointers to items. The user program may release memory occupied by the deleted item, since it is no longer part of the tree.

Returns

a pointer to the parent of the deleted item; NULL, if no match was found.

Related functions

`tfind, tsearch, twalk`

telldir

R3

```
long telldir (DIR *dirp);
```

Headers

sys/types.h, dirent.h

Returns

the current location of the directory file *dirp*

Warning

The returned value can be used as an argument to a subsequent *seekdir* call. Any alteration of the value may cause unexpected results if subsequently passed to seekdir.

Related functions

closedir, opendir, readdir, rewinddir, seekdir, dirent.h

tempnam

```
char *tempnam (const char *dir, const
    char *prefix);
```

Headers

stdio.h

Tempnam generates a pathname for a temporary file. The directory used is (1) the pathname pointed to by *dir*, if *dir* is not NULL; or (2) the value of $TMPDIR, if defined; or (3) the directory defined by P_tmpdir in stdio.h, if that directory is writable by the caller; otherwise, (4) the /tmp directory.

If *prefix* is not NULL, the filename will be prefixed by the string (up to five characters) pointed to by *prefix*.

The pathname is generated in an area allocated using malloc. The user is responsible for creating and opening the temporary file, and for closing and removing the file after use.

Returns

a pointer to the generated path name; NULL, if `malloc` failed

Warning

Although unlikely, temporary file names generated by other means could duplicate other filenames.

Related functions

`creat, fopen, mktemp, tmpnam, unlink`

tfind

```
void *tfind (void *key, void **root,
   int (*compar)());
```

Headers

`search.h`

`Tfind` searches a binary tree for an item matching *key*. *Root* must point to a pointer that in turn points to the tree's root node; if **root* is NULL, the tree is considered empty.

The user comparison function *compar*, declared as

```
int compar (void *item1, void
  *item2);
```

must compare *item1* and *item2*, and return an integer value that describes ordering relation between *item1* and *item2* as follows:

When *item1* is equal to, greater than, or less than *item2*, *compar* must return a zero, positive, or negative integer value, respectively.

`Tfind` is similar to `tsearch` except that `tfind` does not insert item into tree if it is not found.

Returns

a pointer to the tree node matching *key*; NULL if no match is found. A node contains a pointer to the actual item.

Related functions

`tdelete, tsearch, twalk`

time

errno S

```
time_t time (time_t *buf):
```

Headers

`sys/types.h`

Returns

the current value of the system time-of-day clock. If *buf* is not NULL, the clock value is also stored in *buf*.

The clock value is the number of seconds elapsed since midnight GMT, January 1, 1970.

Related functions

`stime`

tmpfile

```
FILE *tmpfile (void);
```

Headers

`stdio.h`

A temporary file is created in the directory defined as `P_tmpdir` in `stdio.h` and is opened for both reading and writing ("w+"). It is automatically deleted when the calling process terminates.

Returns

pointer to open FILE block; NULL pointer, if file could not be opened

Related functions

`mktemp, tmpnam, tmpname`

tmpnam

```
char *tmpnam (char *buf);
```

Headers

`stdio.h`

`Tmpnam` generates a temporary file name. The pathname is stored in a user buffer of at least `L_tmpnam` bytes pointed to by *buf* or, if *buf* is the NULL pointer, in an internal static area.

The user is responsible for creating and opening the file, and for deleting the file after use.

Returns

a pointer to the generated pathname

Warning

The generated filename can duplicate the name of another file in the `P_tmpdir` directory, but names are chosen in a manner highly likely to be unique.

Related functions

`creat, fopen, mktemp, tempnam, tmpfile, unlink`

toascii

```
int toascii (int ch);
```

The value of *ch* is converted to an ASCII character code by setting bits of *ch* to 0 that are always 0 in ASCII.

tolower

```
int tolower (int ch);
```

Returns

the lowercase equivalent of `ch`, if any.

Related functions

`_tolower, toupper`

toupper

```
int toupper (int ch);
```

Returns

the uppercase equivalent of `ch`, if any.

Related functions

`_toupper, tolower`

tsearch

```
void *tsearch (void *key, void **root,
   int (*compar)());
```

Headers

`search.h`

`Tsearch` searches a binary tree for the item pointed to by *key*, inserts the item if it is not present, and returns a pointer to the node containing the item. The object pointed to by *key* may contain any kind of data; `tsearch` does not examine the contents of an item.

Compar points to a user function:

```
int compar (void *item1, void *item2);
```

When *item1* is equal to, greater than, or less than *item2*, *compar* must return a zero, positive, or negative integer value, respectively.

Root must point to the root node of the binary tree. If the value of **root* is NULL, the tree is considered empty. The value of **root* may be changed by `tsearch` and `tdelete`.

Returns

a pointer to the matching node; node contains a pointer to the item. Returns NULL if space could not be allocated.

Warning

Tsearch does not copy inserted items; the tree contains only pointers to items. Therefore, the user must preserve an item until it is deleted explicitly by `tdelete`.

Related functions

`bsearch, hsearch, lsearch, tdelete, tfind, twalk`

ttyname

```
char *ttyname (int handle);
```

Returns

a pointer to a string in an internal static area, giving the pathname of the terminal on which the file descriptor *handle* is open; or NULL if the device corresponding to *handle* is not a terminal.

Related functions

`ctermid, isatty`

twalk

```
void twalk (void *item, void
    (*action)());
```

Headers

`stdio.h`

Use `twalk` to traverse a binary tree as built by `tsearch`, or any subtree of a tree.

Item pointer must point to a node of the tree (root node or any node below it). The node and all its subordinate nodes will be traversed.

The user function pointed to by *action* will be called for each node as it is visited. The function declaration is

```
void action (void **item, VISIT
  order, int depth);
```

where *item* is a pointer to node of the tree, and *order* is one of the enumeration values

```
typedef enum { preorder, postorder,
   endorder, leaf } VISIT;
```

Order indicates for which visit of the node the user routine has been called. (Each node is visited three times: *preorder* visit occurs before any child nodes are visited; *postorder* visit occurs after left child and before visiting the right; *endorder* visit occurs after visiting both children.) *Depth* indicates node's depth relative to starting node.

`Twalk` returns when node pointed to by *item* and all its child nodes have been visited.

Related functions

`tdelete, tfind, tsearch`

tzset

```
void tzset (void);
   extern long timezone;
   extern char *tzname[2];
   extern int  daylight;
```

Headers

time.h

`Tzset` is called by `asctime` to update the variables *timezone*, *tzname*, and *daylight*.

Timezone specifies the number of seconds to be added to Greenwich mean time (GMT) to obtain the local time.

Positive values indicate western time zones; negative values indicate eastern time zones.

Tzname points to an array of two pointers to strings.

The first element gives the name of the local standard time zone, while the second gives the name of the local daylight saving time zone.

Daylight contains 1 (*TRUE*) when a daylight saving time conversion should be applied to obtain the local time; 0 (*FALSE*) otherwise.

The contents of these variables is derived from the TZ environment string, in the format

```
SSS[-]hhDDD
```

where `SSS` is the name of the local standard time zone, `[-]` denotes an optional minus sign, `hh` specifies the number of hours to be added to GMT, and `DDD` is the name of the local daylight saving time zone.

Related functions

asctime

ulimit

errno S

```
long ulimit (int cmd, long newlimit);
```

One of the process limits as specified by *cmd* is returned or set to *newlimit*. The following are possible values of *cmd*:

1 Get the file size limit. Returns maximum number of 512-byte blocks that can be written to any one file by the calling process.

2 Set file size limit. Limit may be adjusted upward only if effective user-ID is super-user.

3 Get maximum possible break address.

Returns

requested value; –1 if an error occurred.

umask

S

```
int umask (int mask);
```

The process file-creation mask is set to *mask*. The mask modifies the nine low-order bits of the access permissions when creating a new file. Bits set to one in *mask* cause the corresponding access-permission bit of the new file to be set to zero.

The process file-creation mask is inherited by all child processes.

Returns

previous value of file-creation mask

Related functions

`chmod, creat, mknod, open`

uname

errno S

```
int uname (struct utsname *buf);
```

Headers

`sys/utsname.h`

The current operating system identification is stored in the structure pointed to by *buf*. Members of the structure are character strings. The information returned includes:

`sysname`	Name of current UNIX system
`nodename`	System namein a UUCP network
`release`	Release of active operating system
`version`	Version of active operating system
`machine`	Type of CPU being used

Generally, there are no standards for the format of information returned.

ungetc

```
int ungetc (int c, FILE *stream);
```

Headers

`stdio.h`

Use `ungetc` to push a character back onto the input file *stream*. The next standard input call will return the character *c* before reading *stream*.

Returns

value of *c*; EOF, if push could not be performed

Warning

Pushing cannot be performed if *stream* is unbuffered, if no input has yet been read, or if an `ungetc` has already been performed without an intervening `getc`. `Fseek` destroys the effect of `ungetc`.

Related functions

`fseek, getc, setbuf`

unlink

errno S

```
int unlink (const char *path);
```

The directory entry for *path* is removed if the calling process has write access to the directory containing the entry or is effectively a super-user, and the entry is not the last link for a file currently being executed, or the mount point for a currently mounted file system. If the removed directory entry was the last link to a file, the file will be removed.

Returns

0 if successful; –1 otherwise

Related functions

`link, mknod`

utime

errno S

```
int utime (const char *path, struct
    {time_t actime, mtime;} *times);
```

Headers

`sys/types.h`

If *times* is the NULL pointer, access and modification times of the file named by *path* are set to the current time. The calling process must be the file owner or have write permission.

If *times* is not NULL, access and modification times are set to values of *actime* and *mtime* contained in *times*.

Times are expressed as the number of seconds elapsed since midnight Greenwich mean time (GMT), January 1, 1970. Calling process must have an effective user-ID equal to the owner-ID of file, or must be super-user.

Returns

0 if successful; –1 otherwise

Related functions

`stat, time`

va_arg

```
type va_arg (va_list list, type);
```

Headers

`varargs.h`

Use `va_arg` to retrieve the next argument from a variable-length argument list. The argument to be retrieved is presumed to be of type *type*; *list* is incremented by the size of a *type* variable so that the next argument can be accessed. `Va_start` must have been executed prior to invocation of `va_arg`.

Returns

value of next argument.

Warning

Function arguments are passed on the stack (stored one after the other in a contiguous area of storage). If the size in bytes implied by *type* does not match the actual size of an argument, the pointer will be set incorrectly for the next use of `va_arg`. The caller must ensure that *type* agrees with the actual type of the arguments.

Related functions

`va_end, va_start`

va_end

```
void va_end (va_list list);
```

Headers

varargs.h

`Va_end` is used with `va_start` to access unknown arguments of a function. Code the `va_end` macro at the end of a range of instructions where `va_arg` is used.

Warning

The range of a `va_start-va_end` bracket may not extend beyond the code block containing `va_start`.

Related functions

`va_arg, va_start`

va_start

```
void va_start (va_list list, arg);
```

Headers

varargs.h

Use the `va_start` macro to access undeclared function arguments. *List* is initialized to point to the argument named *arg*. Arguments following *arg* can be retrieved by repeated calls to `va_arg`. When the last argument has been accessed, `va_end` must be invoked to properly terminate `varargs` processing.

Non-ANSI compilers use the following format:

```
va_start (list);
```

list names a variable of type `va_list` which is initialized to refer to the argument represented by *va_alist* in the function declaration; *va_alist* must be declared to be of type *va_dcl*, with no ending semicolon. For example:

```
int vprintf (format, va_alist)
char *format;
va_dcl {
        va_list args;
        char *strptr;
        va_start(args);
        strptr = va_arg(args, char *);
        va_end(args);
}
```

Warning

The user is responsible for properly determining the type of an undeclared argument.

Related functions

va_arg, va_end

vfprintf

errno

```
int vfprintf (FILE *stream, const char
    *format, va_list args);
```

Headers

stdio.h, varargs.h

Vfprintf functions the same as fprintf except the list of arguments is supplied as varargs pointer. This form of fprintf typically is useful when the list of arguments passed to a user-written function are in turn to be processed as arguments of fprintf.

Returns

number of characters written to *stream*; EOF on error

Related functions

fprintf, printf, sprintf, va_start, vprintf

vprintf

errno

```
int vprintf (const char *format,
   va_list args);
```

Headers

`stdio.h, varargs.h`

`Vprintf` functions the same as `printf` except the list of arguments is supplied as varargs pointer. This form of `printf` is useful when a list of arguments passed to a user-written function are in turn to be processed as arguments of `printf`.

Returns

number of characters written to standard output; negative number on error.

Related functions

`fprintf, printf, sprintf, va_start, vfprintf`

wait

errno S

```
int wait (int *status);
```

`Wait` allows a parent process to wait for completion of its child processes. If the calling process has no children, –1 is returned and *errno* is set to ECHILD. Otherwise, the calling process is suspended until one of its child processes terminates or a signal is received. If a signal is received and caught, `wait` returns –1 and *errno* indicates EINTR. This does not indicate termination of the child process; `wait` should be repeated.

When a child process terminates, status information is stored in the 16 low-order bits of *status*, and `wait` returns the process-ID of the child process. *Status* indicates one of the following:

- Normal termination. The eight low-order bits of status are zero; the high-order bits contain the exit value of child process.
- Termination by signal. The seven low-order bits of status contain the signal number, and the 0200 bit is set if a core file was written. The high-order bits of status are zero.
- Termination due to a trace condition. The high-order bits identify trace condition; the low-order eight bits are set to 0177.

Returns

the process-ID of the child process that has terminated; –1 if an error occurred.

Warning

1. If signal SIGCLD (death of a child) is set to *func*, `wait` will always indicate EINTR.
2. There is no way to wait selectively for termination of a specific child process; `wait` will return for the next child process that terminates.

Related functions

`exit, fork, pause, signal`

write

errno S

```
int write (int handle, void *buf,
   unsigned len);
```

Bytes of the character array pointed to by *buf* are written in left-to-right order to the file *handle* until *len* bytes are written, a capacity limit is reached, or an error occurs.

For block-special files, writing begins at the next byte in the file or at an offset specified by `lseek`, except that if the file descriptor specifies O_APPEND, the file pointer is set to EOF before writing begins. For character-special files and pipes, `lseek` has no effect.

Returns

the number of bytes actually written; –1 on error.

Related functions

`creat, fcntl, lseek, open, pipe, ulimit`

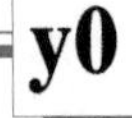

y0

errno -lm

```
double y0 (double x);
```

Headers

`math.h`

Returns

Bessel function of the second kind, of order 0, corresponding to argument *x*. The function is defined for positive values of *x*; other values cause a *matherr* condition to be recognized.

y1

errno -lm

```
double y1 (double x);
```

Headers

`math.h`

Returns

Bessel function of the second kind, of order 1, corresponding to argument *x*. The function is defined for positive values of *x*; other values cause a *matherr* condition to be recognized.

yn

errno -lm

```
double yn (double x);
```

Headers

math.h

Returns

Bessel function of the second kind, of order *n*, corresponding to argument *x*. The function is defined for positive values of *x*; other values cause a *matherr* condition to be recognized.

Principal Data Structures

Each important structure that must be constructed or examined by System V function users is described in this section. Data areas internal to UNIX are not listed here, since they cannot be referenced directly. When the structures described here are used, portability is maintained across implementations of System V.

dir.h

```
#define DIRSIZ  ...
struct  direct {
        ino_t   d_ino;
        char    d_name[DIRSIZ];
};
```

Headers

sys/types.h

A *directory* is a file consisting of *n* equal-length records. Each record contains the name of a file in the directory (*d_name*) and an i-node number (*d_ino*) that identifies the object to which the directory entry points. The filename is padded with null characters to a length of DIRSIZ (but note that a maximum-length file name is not null-terminated). If the i-node number is zero, the entry has previously been removed, and the filename field is not meaningful.

A directory can be read by a user program using functions such as `read` or `fread` but cannot be written unless the process is effectively a super-user.

Warning

The size of a directory entry and the maximum length of an entry's file name are implementation-dependent.

dirent.h

R3

```
#define MAXNAMLEN
    typedef struct {
            int      dd_fd;
            int      dd_loc;
            int      dd_size;
            char     *dd_buf;
     } DIR;
     struct dirent {
            long               d_ino;
            off_t              d_off;
            unsigned short d_reclen;
            char               d_name[1];
     };
```

Headers

`sys/types.h dirent.h`

UNIX directory files contain pointers to other files, namely its members. While directories are simple in structure, entry formats may differ between versions of System V Release 3.2 provides functions and headers that support directory access in a portable fashion.

`Opendir` returns a pointer to a structure of type `DIR` that is used like `FILE` for stream I/O. A declaration of this struct is provided in `dirent.h`. `Readdir` returns a pointer to a `dirent` struct containing a directory entry in system-independent format. The principal members of `struct dirent` follow:

`d_ino`	i-node number of the file
`d_off`	byte offset of the corresponding directory entry from the start of the directory
`d_reclen`	length of the directory entry
`d_name[1]`	character array containing the filename.

The maximum filename length is MAXNAMLEN.

Warning

`d_reclen` is not the length of `d_name`; it is used internally by directory-access functions.

Related structures and functions

`closedir, opendir, readdir, rewinddir, seekdir, telldir`

pwd.h

```
struct passwd {
        char     *pw_name;
        char     *pw_passwd;
        int       pw_uid;
        int       pw_gid;
        char     *pw_age;
        char     *pw_comment;
        char     *pw_gecos;
        char     *pw_dir;
        char     *pw_shell;
};
```

The `passwd` structure is used by various functions to display the contents of a line of the `/etc/passwd` file. The struct contains at least the following members:

`pw_name`	points to character string of at most `L_cuserid` characters (defined in `stdio.h`). String is login name of user described by this entry.
`pw_passwd`	points to character string, of at most 13 characters, containing encrypted password. String may be empty, if no password is defined for this user, value of *pw_passwd* may be NULL pointer.
`pw_uid`	contains integer user-ID for this user.
`pw_gid`	contains integer group-ID for this user.
`pw_comment`	is not used.
`pw_gecos`	points to arbitrary string commonly used for user ID or accounting.
`pw_dir`	points to path of user's home directory.
`pw_shell`	points to name of user's login shell. If not specified, `/bin/sh` is used.

Related structures and functions

`endpwent, fgetpwent, getpwent, getpwuid, getpwnam, setpwent`

search.h

```
/* HSEARCH */
typedef struct entry { const void
   *key, *data; } ENTRY;
typedef enum { FIND, ENTER } ACTION;
/* TSEARCH */
typedef enum { preorder, postorder,
   endorder, leaf } VISIT;
```

`Search.h` defines data structures used by `hsearch` and `tsearch`.

shadow.h

R3

```
define PASSWD     "/etc/passwd"
#define SHADOW    "/etc/shadow"
#define OPASSWD   "/etc/opasswd"
#define OSHADOW   "/etc/oshadow"
#define PASSTEMP  "/etc/ptmp"
#define SHADTEMP  "/etc/stmp"
#define DAY       (24L * 60 * 60)
#define DAY_NOW   (long)time((long *)0)
                  / DAY
struct spwd {
           char  *sp_namp;
           char  *sp_pwdp;
           long  sp_lstchg;
           long  sp_min;
           long  sp_max;
};
```

Beginning with System V Release 3.2 password information is not returned in `struct passwd;` instead, `pw_passwd` points to the string "x", and the password can be obtained only by a shadow password function.

The `getspent`, `fgetspent`, or `getspnam` functions return an `spwd` structure containing:

`sp_namp`	pointer to user name string
`sp_pwdp`	pointer to the password string
`sp_lstchg`	date password was last changed
`sp_min`	minimum number of days before the password can be changed again
`sp_max`	number of days after which the password must be changed

Warning

The effective user-ID must be super-user to invoke the shadow password functions. The `-lsec` option must be passed to `cc` to link shadow password functions.

Related structures and functions

endpwent, getpwent, getpwnam, putpwent, setpwent

stat.h

```
struct stat {
     ushort  st_mode;
     ino_t   st_ino;
     dev_t   st_dev;
     dev_t   st_rdev;
     short   st_nlink;
     ushort  st_uid;
     ushort  st_gid;
     off_t   st_size;
     time_t  st_atime;
     time_t  st_mtime;
     time_t  st_ctime;
};
```

Headers

sys/types.h

The_stat structure is returned by stat and fstat. Members of the structure are extracted from the file's i-node and describe its characteristics. At least the following members are defined:

st_mode	Describes type of file and file-access permissions. Symbolic values are defined in sys/stat.h for examining individual bit fields of mode(see table 7).
st_ino	Index of i-node in i-node table.
st_dev	For disk files, a code uniquely identifying file system containing file.
st_rdev	For block-special and character-special files only, major and minor device numbers of associated device.

Table 7. File mode flags

Name	*Value*	*Meaning*
S_IFMT	0170000	File type subfield
S_IFREG	0100000	Regular
S_IFBLK	0060000	Block special
S_IFDIR	0040000	Directory
S_IFCHR	0020000	Character special
S_IFIFO	0010000	Fifo (named pipe)
S_ISUID	04000	Set user-ID on execution
S_ISGID	02000	Set group-ID on execution
S_ISVTX	01000	Save text image (tacky bit)
S_IREAD	00400	Read permission for owner
S_IWRITE	00200	Write permission for owner
S_IEXEC	00100	Execute/search owner permission
—	00040	Read permission for group
—	00020	Write permission for group
—	00010	Execute/search group permission
—	00004	Read permission for others
—	00002	Write permission for others
—	00001	Execute/search others' permission

Values are combined by using bitwise-OR operation.

`st_nlink`	Number of links to this file or device.
`st_uid`	User-ID of file's owner.
`st_gid`	Group-ID of file's group.
`st_size`	Size of file in bytes.
`st_atime`	Clock value of last file access.
`st_mtime`	Clock value of last file change.
`st_ctime`	Clock value of last i-node entry change.

Warning

St_dev and *st_rdev* are intended primarily for operating-system use; their meaning may vary from one implementation, version, or release of UNIX to another.

Related structures and functions

`chmod`, `ctime`, `fstat`, `gmtime`, `link`, `localtime`, `mknod`, `stat`, `time`, `unlink`

time.h

```
struct tm {
      int tm_sec;    /* seconds */
      int tm_min;    /* minutes */
      int tm_hour;   /* hours */
      int tm_mday;   /* day of month */
      int tm_mon;    /* month */
      int tm_year;   /* year - 1900 */
      int tm_wday;   /* day of week */
      int tm_yday;   /* day of year */
      int tm_isdst;  /* Daylight
                  savings time flag */
};
```

The `tm` struct is returned by `localtime` and `gmtime`. Its members describe the components of a time-of-day clock value. At least the following members are defined:

`tm_sec`	Contains *seconds* portion of time of day as an integer in the range 0-59.
`tm_min`	Contains *minutes* portion of time of day as an integer in the range 0-59.
`tm_hour`	Contains *hours* portion of time of day as an integer in the range 0-23.
`tm_mday`	Contains day of month. (First day is *1*).
`tm_wday`	Contains day of week as an integer in the range 0-6. Value *0* corresponds to *Sunday*.
`tm_yday`	Contains numeric day of year. First day of year is *0*; last day is *364* (*365* if leap year).
`tm_mon`	Contains month as an integer from 0-11. Add 1 if value is to be printed directly.
`tm_year`	Contains year as number elapsed since 1970. Add 70 or 1970 to print value directly.
`tm_isdst`	Contains value *1* if date falls in period corresponding to daylight savings time for year *tm_year*; otherwise, value is *0*.

Warning

Daylight-savings computation is unreliable unless it corresponds to years for which function was programmed.

Function Finder

In this topical index, commonly used functions are listed first, then less frequently used or specialized functions.

^ = functions introduced in R3 of System V

Character handling

Change case	`tolower, toupper, _tolower, _toupper`
Compare byte	`strcmp, strncmp, memcmp`
Copy bytes	`strcpy, strcat, strdup^, strncat, strncpy, memccpy, memcpy`
Fill bytes	`memset`
Find character	`strchr, strrchr, memchr`
Find substring	`strtok, strspn, strcspn, strpbrk`
Force valid ASCII	`toascii`
Length of string	`strlen`
Test character type	`isalnum, isalpha, isascii, iscntrl, isdigit, isgraph, islower, isprint, ispunct, isspace, isupper, isxdigit`

Conversions

ASCII to integer	`atoi`
ASCII to long	`atol strtol`
ASCII to float	`atof strtod`

Float to ASCII	`ecvt, fcvt, gcvt`
Internal to string	`sprintf`
String to internal	`sscanf`

Date and time

Read system clock	`time`
Set time zone	`tzset`
Decode clock value	`ctime, localtime, gmtime`
Measure elapsed time	`clock`
Print `tm` struct	`asctime`
Test time zone	`daylight, timezone, tzname`

Directories

Create directory	`mkdir^`
Open directory	`opendir^`
Close directory	`closedir^`
Delete directory	`rmdir^`
Position to entry	`rewinddir^, seekdir^, telldir^`
Read entry	`readdir^`
Walk directory tree	`ftw`

File administration

Create alias filename	`link`
Create temp filenames	`mktemp, tempnam, tmpnam`
Delete file	`unlink`
Get file status	`stat, fstat`
Set ownership	`chown`
Set permissions	`chmod`
Set date and time	`utime`
Test access permission	`access`

File input/output

Close file	`close`
Control file	`ioctl, fcntl`
Copy file descriptor	`dup, fcntl`

Lock for exclusive use	`lockf, fcntl`
Open file	`open, creat, pipe`
Read bytes	`read`
Set position	`lseek`
Write bytes	`write`

Mathematical functions

Absolute value	`abs, fabs`
Bessel functions	`j0, j1, jn, y0, y1, yn`
Error function	`erf, erfc`
Gamma function	`gamma`
Hyperbolic functions	`cosh, sinh, tanh`
Hypotenuse	`hypot`
Logarithms	`exp, log, log10`
Parts of number	`modf`
Powers and roots	`pow, sqrt`
Random numbers	`rand, srand, drand48, erand48, jrand48, lcong48, lrand48, mrand48, nrand48, seed48, srand48`
Rounding	`ceil, floor, fmod`
Trigonometric functions	`acos, asin, atan, atan2, cos, sin, tan`

Memory management

Allocate memory	`malloc, realloc, calloc`
Control allocation	`mallopt, mallinfo`
Free memory	`free`
Test memory size	`edata, end, etext`

Passwords

Read password	`getpass`

Process control

Create process	`fork`
Execute program	`system, popen, pclose, execl, execle, execlp, execv, execve, execvp`

Exit program	`exit, abort, _exit`
Get current directory	`getcwd`
Get environment	`getenv, environ`
Get group-ID	`getgid, getegid`
Get process-ID	`getpid, getppid, getpgrp`
Get user-ID	`getuid, geteuid, cuserid, getlogin, logname`
Monitor execution	`monitor, profil`
Print error message	`perror, sys_errlist, sys_nerr`
Set current directory	`chdir`
Set environment	`putenv`
Set file-creation mask	`umask`
Set identity	`setuid, setgid, setpgrp`
Set limits	`ulimit`
Set priority	`nice`
Set signal handling	`signal`
Signal a process	`kill, alarm`
Test cause of error	`errno`
Wait for event	`wait, pause, sleep`

Programming aids

Insert debugging code	`assert`
Jump out of function	`longjmp, setjmp`
Parse command options	`getopt`
Variable argument lists	`va_arg, va_end, va_start`

Stream files

Clear errors	`clearerr`
Open stream	`fopen, fdopen, freopen`
Open temp file	`tmpfile`
Close stream	`fclose`
Flush output buffer	`fflush`

Get handle of stream	`fileno`
Read character	`getchar, getc, fgetc`
Read integers	`getw`
Read string	`fgets, gets`
Read data	`scanf, fscanf, fread`
Set buffering mode	`setbuf, setvbuf`
Write character	`putchar, putc, fputc`
Write integers	`putw`
Write string	`puts, fputs`
Write data	`printf, fprintf, vprintf, vfprintf, fwrite`
Position file	`rewind, fseek, ftell`
Test for error	`feof, ferror`
Unget character	`ungetc`

Sorting and searching

Binary search	`bsearch`
Hash search	`hcreate, hdestroy, hsearch`
Linear search	`lfind, lsearch`
Tree search	`tsearch, tdelete, tfind, twalk`
Quick sort	`qsort`

System administration

Get system name	`uname`
`/etc/passwd` file access	`endpwent, getpwent, getpwnam, getpwuid, setpwent`

Terminal

Control interface	`ioctl`
Get file name of	`ctermid, ttyname`
Test for	`isatty`